10-MINUTE IDEAS
FOR EARLY YEARS

Alphabet fun

Jillian Harker

■ **Quick activities for any time of the day**

■ **Links to Early Learning Goals** ■ **Time-saving photocopiables**

Credits

Author
Jillian Harker

Editor
Lesley Sudlow

Assistant Editor
Jennifer Shiels

Series Designer
Anna Oliwa

Designer
Andrea Lewis

Cover Illustration
Craig Cameron/Art
Collection

Illustrations
Bethan Matthews/
Sylvie Poggio
Artists Agency

Text © 2004
© 2004 Scholastic Ltd

Designed using Adobe InDesign

Published by Scholastic Ltd
Villiers House
Clarendon Avenue
Leamington Spa
Warwickshire
CV32 5PR

www.scholastic.co.uk

Printed by Bell & Bain

1 2 3 4 5 6 7 8 9   4 5 6 7 8 9 0 1 2 3

British Library Cataloguing-in-Publication Data
A catalogue record for this book is available from the British Library.

ISBN 0-439-97643-X

Contents

Contents

Physical development

Creative development

Photocopiables

Introduction

Language, both spoken and written, is the foundation that underpins all learning. The activities in this book are designed to help young children develop the alphabet skills that are central to the ability to master the written forms of our language. The aim is to provide early years practitioners with new ideas for teaching the alphabet.

'Learning the alphabet' is often viewed as a limited task, with activities frequently focussing on pencil and paper exercises before necessary underlying skills are in place. This book takes a broader-based approach, covering skills such as the discrimination of sounds within words, the link between sounds and letters, the perception of rhyme and alliteration, early writing skills and the reading of simple words.

The activites range across all six Areas of Learning, as described in the document *Curriculum Guidance for the Foundation Stage* (QCA), an approach based in the belief that every Area of Learning provides opportunities to teach and reinforce alphabet skills. By structuring the book in this way, it is intended to promote understanding of the fact that young children need to bring many underlying skills to what is, in reality, a very complex task. In order to read and write the alphabet and simple words, children have to master mathematical skills such as concepts of size and shape; they have to develop the physical skills needed to manipulate writing tools and they must be able to hear similarities and differences between sounds in spoken words.

Teaching alphabetical skills through a range of Areas of Learning taps into young children's natural learning mode. They do not separate off one area of learning from another, so the activities in this book will allow children to explore the sound, shape and size of letters and experiment with rhyme and alliteration within a wider context, at the same time developing, for example, their mathematical, creative or physical skills.

The activities are also intended to be fun. Just as young children can effectively learn a variety of skills through play and experimentation, for example, with sand and water, they can equally acquire a range of skills when they play and experiment with language.

This approach makes for a multi-sensory learning experience, in which children take in information through all of their senses. It not only provides a positive, effective learning experience, but it also means that the different learning styles of a range of children are catered for and so each individual child can learn the way that suits them best.

Using the activities

The main aim of the book is to provide activities that can be carried out in short periods of time, with minimal preparation and using resources that are likely to be found in any early years setting. Where an activity requires a resource such as illustrations, that might be time-consuming to produce, the activity is supported by one or more photocopiable sheets.

Optimum group sizes are given for each activity. With one or two exceptions, the number of children can be varied, but the number suggested will allow the children to obtain maximum benefit from that activity. Step-by-step guidance is provided to enable practitioners to carry out the activity successfully, with additional advice for supporting younger children and extension ideas for older children. Each activity includes a 'Further ideas' section that presents other suggestions for targeting the relevant Stepping Stone.

Stepping Stones and Early Learning Goals

Each chapter focuses on one of the six Areas of Learning, and activities within each chapter are graded, so that those towards the end of the chapter generally require greater skill than those featured earlier on. Each activity is linked to a particular Stepping Stone and Early Learning Goal, both of which are clearly indicated. This is intended to assist practitioners with their planning, helping them to ensure that the learning opportunities that they provide for their children cover a broad range of Stepping Stones and Early Learning Goals.

It is worth noting that, although the Stepping Stones and Early Learning Goals given relate to the Area of Learning being addressed by each particular chapter, all of the activities in this book meet the requirements for Communication, language and literacy.

Assessing the activities

The suggestions that are included in each activity for supporting younger children and extending it for older children, can also provide useful indicators when assessing the children. A child who is managing an activity without the additional support, or who is clearly benefiting from the extension ideas, can be viewed as having achieved the appropriate Stepping Stone. Those who are evidently still in need of support to carry out the activity can be considered as not yet having mastered that particular Stepping Stone. Smaller group activities provide practitioners with an opportunity to assess how well a child has understood and mastered a concept.

How to use this book

The acquisition of alphabet skills will best be achieved through regular short bouts of practice and the activities in this book are designed with this in mind. Larger group activities such as 'Name game' on page 7, 'Sweet and savoury' on page 9 and 'Sound pairs' on page 10 are ideally suited to introduce concepts, for example, alliteration, and to familiarise children with them. Smaller group activities, such as 'Hide-and-seek' on page 68, allow for more focussed individual practice, and also provide an assessment opportunity, permitting practitioners to observe and monitor individual children.

Personal, social and emotional development

The activities in this chapter encourage children to approach new experiences with confidence, be sensitive to the needs, views and feelings of other people while working in groups, and to show care and concern for all living things.

Name game

What you need
Just the children.

What to do
Invite the children to sit in a circle and tell them that they are going to play a 'silly name' game.

Explain to the children that you are going to ask each of them, in turn, to tell you their name. Say that they should tell you their proper first name but that you want them to change their second name into something silly, for example, say, 'If your name is Sarah, then I would like you to choose a silly second name that begins with the same sound as Sarah. You could tell me that your name is Sarah Sausages. Can you hear that "Sarah" and "Sausages" both start with the same sound?' Say that they must all choose a silly second name that begins with the same sound as their first name.

Tell the children that you are going to give them a few minutes to think of a silly name for themselves.

Now invite a child to begin the game and move around the circle, encouraging each child to tell you their silly name.

Support and extension
Before giving younger children time to think up a silly name, check that they can tell you the initial sound of their first name. Challenge older children to think of a silly name from a category such as foods, animals or vegetables.

Further ideas
■ Encourage the children to work together to make a list of animals that begin with the same sound as each child's name, such as 'kangaroo', 'kitten' and 'koala' for 'Katy'. Then let each child talk about which of those animals they would like to have for a pet, if they could choose.
■ Introduce the children to a new soft toy. Have a 'Name the toy' competition, but only let the children suggest names beginning with one or two letters of the alphabet each day. Work through the alphabet, making a list of all the suggested names. After a couple of weeks invite the children to vote for their favourite name.

LEARNING OBJECTIVES
STEPPING STONE
Have a positive approach to new experiences.

EARLY LEARNING GOAL
Be confident to try new activities, initiate ideas and speak in a familiar group.

GROUP SIZE
Any size

HOME LINKS
Explain the 'silly names' game to parents and carers and ask them to help their children think up some silly second names that begin with the same sound as the first names of family members.

Rhyming rules

What you need
Just the children.

What to do
Discuss with the children how having rules about our behaviour can help people to get on with one another. Ask them about any rules that they have at home.

Tell them that you are going to read them some rules that have been written in a rhyme. Say that you will only say the first sound of the last word and you would like them to guess what the word might be. Remind them that it has to make a rhyme.

Read each of the rules in turn and encourage the children to say the last word. Repeat the children's suggestions for them to hear if they rhyme and make sense.

> *It really isn't right*
> *to squabble and to f....*
>
> *You really ought to go to bed*
> *at the time your mum has s...*
>
> *It is kind to share your games and toys*
> *with other girls and other b...*

Discuss each rule with the children and talk about why they think they should behave in this particular way.

Support and extension
Suggest several alternative words for younger children to say for the last word. Try each one out in the rule so that they can listen for the one that rhymes. Leave out the first sound of the last word with older children and ask them to make suggestions for rhyming words that would be appropriate.

Further ideas
■ Make up some more rules, suggest the first lines and let the children complete them. Work together to make the endings rhyme, for example:

> *Do not be unkind to your sister or brother*
> *Try to be kind to one an.....*
>
> *If you have had enough and do not want to play,*
> *Always put your things aw..*

■ Give the children alliterative alternatives such as 'helpful/horrid', 'nasty/nice', 'rude/reasonable', 'selfish/sensible'. Discuss the meaning of the words and talk about which ones would be the best way to be and why.

LEARNING OBJECTIVES
STEPPING STONE
Show care and concern for others, for living things and the environment.

EARLY LEARNING GOAL
Understand what is right, what is wrong and why.

GROUP SIZE
Any size.

HOME LINKS
Send a list of the rhyming rules home, explaining to parents and carers what you have discussed and suggest that they might like to decide with their children which of the rules would be good for their family.

Sweet and savoury

What you need
Just the children.

What to do
Tell the children that you are going to read them a poem about food. Say that there are two interesting things to notice about the foods that are mentioned in each line of the poem, so you would like them to listen very carefully. Read the following poem to the children:

> *Custard with cabbage,*
> *chocolate with cheese,*
> *marmalade and mushrooms,*
> *peaches with peas.*
> *One very interesting thing that I have found*
> *is that I just like foods*
> *that start with the same sound.*

Ask the children what the interesting thing was that was mentioned in the last line of the rhyme. Invite them to listen again to the pairs of food mentioned and encourage them to check that the two items begin with the same sound. Invite them to tell you what each sound is.

Now discuss if these foods would really taste good together. Explore whether any of the children like to eat strange combinations of food together and whether they prefer to eat savoury or sweet things.

Support and extension
With younger children, pause at the end of each line in the rhyme and draw their attention to the two food words, emphasising the initial sound. Then read it through at normal speed. When reading the rhyme to older children, pause after, 'I just like foods that...' and ask if they can suggest what the ending might be.

Further ideas
■ Choose a letter of the alphabet and ask the children to think of foods that begin with that letter. Make a list and invite them to suggest combinations that they would like and others that they would not like.
■ Suggest a feeling that begins with each letter of the alphabet, such as 'anxious', 'brave', 'curious', 'daring', 'excited' and so on. Talk about the meaning of more difficult words and ask the children if they have ever felt like that. (Use 'exhausted' for 'x'.)

LEARNING OBJECTIVES

STEPPING STONE
Express needs and feelings in appropriate ways.

EARLY LEARNING GOAL
Have a developing awareness of their own needs, views and feelings and be sensitive to the needs, views and feelings of others.

GROUP SIZE
Any size.

HOME LINKS
Send the rhyme home for parents and carers to share with their children and suggest that they use it as a basis to talk about their children's favourite and least favourite foods.

Sound pairs

What you need
Just the children.

What to do
Tell the children that you are going to give them two food words that we use a lot together, for example, 'bread and butter'. Ask how many of the children eat bread and butter and whether they like it.

Now say, 'Do you notice anything about the sound at the beginning of each of those words?'. Repeat the words 'bread' and 'butter', emphasising the initial sound of each. Ask the children if the two sounds are the same.

Encourage the children to think of other foods that go together. If necessary, suggest 'fish and chips' as the next possibility. Again, discuss who has eaten these foods and whether they like them. Then move on to exploring the initial sounds of the two words, asking the children to compare them to see if they are the same.

Repeat this procedure for other food pairs such as 'egg and bacon', 'tea and toast', 'curry and rice', and 'pizza and chips'. Encourage the children to talk freely about why they do not eat particular foods, for example, whether this is the result of taste, culture, allergies and so on.

Support and extension
With younger children, separate out the initial sounds from the words so that they can compare them easily. Ask questions to prompt them to talk about likes, dislikes or cultural differences in food. After a couple of examples, invite older children to suggest their own food pairs to talk about and compare.

Further ideas
■ Focus on things that we commonly use and compare the initial sounds, for example, pen and paper, bucket and spade, cup and saucer, bat and ball and so on. Encourage the children to talk about what we use these things for, and which items they have used and why.
■ List items of clothing and explore which ones begin with the same sound. Include clothing from other cultures such as saris and kilt.

LEARNING OBJECTIVES

STEPPING STONE
Talk freely about their home and community.

EARLY LEARNING GOAL
Have a developing respect for their own cultures and beliefs and those of other people.

GROUP SIZE
Any size.

HOME LINKS
Ask parents and carers to let their children bring in samples of specialist foods to broaden the discussions and promote understanding of differences.

Animal partners

What you need
The photocopiable sheet on page 67; thin card.

Preparation
Copy the photocopiable sheet on to thin card and cut out the pictures.

What to do
Explain to the children that you are going to give each of them a picture of an animal. Tell them that they should look very carefully at their own picture without letting anyone else see it. Shuffle the cards and give one to each child, face down.

Invite the children to turn away and look at their picture. Check that all of the children are sure of the name of the animal on their card.

Ask the children to think about the animal's name and the first sound that they hear in that word. Explain that you would like them to try to find someone else with a picture of an animal that begins with the same sound as theirs.

Suggest that they all move around the group, looking at everyone else's card in turn. Tell the children that it will help them if they say the name of their animal to each other as they look at the pictures. Then they will be able to hear if both words have the same sound at the beginning.

LEARNING OBJECTIVES
STEPPING STONE
Seek out others to share experiences.

EARLY LEARNING GOAL
Form good relationships with adults and peers.

GROUP SIZE
Eight children.

Support and extension
Take younger children to one side and make sure that they know their animal's initial sound. Write the initial letter on the back of the cards so that they can compare these as well. Ask older children to find their partner and then to write the initial letter of the animals on the back of the cards themselves.

Further ideas
■ Encourage partners to look through appropriate books together to see if they can discover other animals that begin with the same sound as theirs.
■ Invite the children to draw simple pictures of rhyming objects such as hat/cat, tin/pin and so on. Ask them to hunt out their favourite rhyming partner and help them to write the rhyming patterns on the back of their cards.

HOME LINKS
Give each child a copy of the photocopiable sheet to take home. Suggest to parents and carers that they cut them up and use them to play a memory game with their children, taking turns to flip over two cards to see if they have a pair with the same initial sound.

Go fetch!

**LEARNING
OBJECTIVES**
STEPPING STONE
Show increasing
independence
in selecting and
carrying out
activities.

**EARLY LEARNING
GOAL**
Continue to be
interested, excited
and motivated to
learn.

GROUP SIZE
Four children.

What you need
Any four wooden or plastic letters; objects with names that begin with each of the four letters.

What to do
Place the four letters on a table and invite the children to join you for a game. Ask each child to pick up a letter and encourage them to think about the sound of this letter.

Explain that you are going to say, 'Go fetch!' and that then they must look around the room for as many things as they can find that begin with the letter that they are holding. Tell them that they must bring the objects back and place them on the table next to their letter. Say that when you say 'Fetch here!', they must stop looking and return to you.

Now say, 'Go fetch!' and allow the children a few minutes to hunt for the objects. When you have called them back and they have displayed their items on the table, ask each child to give you the sound of their letter and to name each of their found objects.

Support and extension
Before younger children set off to hunt, check that they know the sound of their letter and make suggestions as to the sort of objects that they might look for. Alternatively, work as a group to find objects to match each letter in turn. Use letter names with older children or provide two letters for each child.

HOME LINKS
Ask parents and
carers to help their
children hunt around
the house to see
if they can find
something beginning
with each letter of
the alphabet. Explain
the rule about the
letter 'x'.

Further ideas
■ Invite the children to make an inventory of objects in the room in alphabetical order. Let them lay things out beside a large format alphabet line. For the letter 'x', encourage them to find something that ends with this sound, for example 'box'.

■ Pull wooden letters from a bag to indicate where the children should go for their next activity, for example, 's' for sand, 'w' for water and so on.

Which end?

What you need
A4 paper; marker pen; list of simple words with the same sound occurring either at the beginning or the end, for example, 't': tap, ten, hit, tug, pat, hot, bat, tip, tag, hat.

Preparation
On a sheet of A4 paper (landscape), draw three boxes, side by side. Make a photocopy of the sheet for each child.

What to do
Give each child a photocopied sheet of paper with three boxes on. Explain that they are going to play a word game. Tell them that you are going to say a word and you would like them to listen very carefully to work out where they can hear the sound 't' in the word. Encourage the children to point to the box on the left of their sheet if they hear the sound 't' at the beginning of the word, or to point to the box on the right of their sheet If they hear the sound 't' at the end of the word.

Now say, 'Listen for the sound "t". Where does the sound "t" come in the word "top"?'. Check that the children are all pointing to the correct box. Invite a child to tell you where they heard the sound 't', at the beginning or at the end of the word.

Do the same with the word 'pot', then work through your list of words. Let each child say where they heard the target sound in two of the words.

Support and extension
With younger children, separate the target sound out slightly from the word. For older children, introduce words that have the target sound in the middle, for example, letter, butter, pattern and so on, and encourage them to use the middle box on the sheet of paper for these.

Further idea
■ Record sounds and sets of ten words on to a tape. Give each child a sheet of paper with ten sets of three smaller boxes and a pencil. Play the tape and ask them to record the position of the sound in each word by writing a cross in the appropriate box.

Hide-and-seek

What you need
The photocopiable sheet on page 68; thin card.

Preparation
Photocopy the photocopiable sheet on to thin card and then cut out the individual pictures.

What to do
On a table, in two separate groups, lay out the pictures of the animals and the hiding places. Show two children the pictures. Tell them that you would like each of them to hide two of the animals and invite them to choose two animal cards. Say that they must hide the animals under a card showing something that begins with the same sound as the animal name. For example, ask the child that has chosen the bird to tell you the initial sound in the word 'bird'. Encourage them to look at the four hiding places and to place the bird under

something that begins with the same sound. Work through the other cards.

Invite the children to fetch the other two children to look at the hiding places. Ask them to tell these children which animals have been hidden. Explain to the 'seekers' that they must guess where each animal is. Tell them that they will find each animal under a picture that begins with the same sound as the animal name. Invite one of the children to tell you the initial sound in 'bird' and ask them to choose a hiding place beginning with the same sound. Let them check to see if they are correct. Then do the same with the other child and a different animal. Encourage the children to work out the last two animals' hiding places together.

Support and extension
Sound out the animal names and hiding places for younger children, emphasising the initial sounds. You can let older children work out the initial sounds themselves.

Further idea
■ Provide the children with other animal pictures cut from magazines. Invite them to think of alliterative hiding places and to draw these on to cards for further games.

Colour labels

What you need
Post-it notes; selection of red, blue, green, yellow and orange felt-tipped pens for each child.

Preparation
Make sure that there are a variety of red, blue, green, yellow and orange items around the room.

What to do
Give each child five different-coloured felt-tipped pens and five Post-it notes. Tell them that they are going to play a game in which they put labels on things in the room. Explain that they will each have to make their own labels before they can begin to play.

Pick up a red pen and ask the children what colour it is. Invite them to tell you the sound that they can hear at the beginning of the word 'red'. Now say, 'Does anyone know which letter we use to write that sound?'. Encourage the children to name the letter.

Ask the children to write a lower case 'r' in red pen on the first Post-it note. Work through each of the coloured felt-tipped pens, inviting the children to write the initial letter of the colour on a Post-it note each time, in the appropriate colour.

Finally, encourage the children to look again at all five letters and to tell you the colour word starting with each letter. Now invite them to find something in the room of each colour and to stick on the matching Post-it note.

Support and extension
Scribe the letters for younger children. Let older children stick their Post-it notes on objects without checking through the colours again.

Further ideas
■ Play the game using other colours. Make sure that you do not have any duplicate initial letters in the range of colours that you use for any one game.
■ Invite the children to label things according to the material that they are made from, for example, 'w' for wood, 'p' for plastic, 'f' for fabric, 'm' for metal and so on.

LEARNING OBJECTIVES
STEPPING STONE
Take initiatives and manage developmentally appropriate tasks.

EARLY LEARNING GOAL
Select and use activities and resources independently.

GROUP SIZE
Up to five children.

HOME LINKS
Suggest to parents and carers that they help their children to make 'initial' labels for family members. Ask parents and carers to let their children help to sort the washing into piles using the family name labels

Hunt your letter

What you need
Paper; pencils; red pens; section of newsprint in medium-sized letters cut from a newspaper or magazine for each child.

Preparation
Choose the sections of newsprint and cut them out, making sure that there are several examples of each child's initial in the section chosen for them.

What to do
Invite the children to join you at a table and give each child a piece of paper and a pencil. Ask the children to write the first letter of their name as a capital letter. Discuss the shape of each letter and compare each child's initial. Invite them to write the letter again in lower case. Discuss the shape of the letters again. Mix up the sheets of paper and invite the children to find their own sheet again.

Give each child a section of newsprint and a red pen and say that they are going to play a game. Tell them to look very carefully at their piece of print and to see how many times they can find their initial. Say that they should draw a red circle around it each time. Ask them to look for the capital and lower case letter.

Encourage the children to track underneath the letters with their finger. Help them by suggesting that you can see one of their letters in a particular line.

Support and extension
For younger children, write an example of their initial for them. Concentrate on just the capital letter and use large headline newsprint in capital letters for them to look through. Use smaller print and a slightly longer section of newsprint for older children.

Further ideas
■ Write each child's initials on four separate pieces of paper and hide these around the room, then invite the children to find their own initials. Next, ask them to write another child's initial on a piece of paper and to hide it for that child to find.
■ Make a simple game of 'Letter lotto' with four letters on each baseboard. Encourage the children to cover matching letters with counters as you pull wooden letters out of a bag.

Communication, language and literacy

This chapter provides ideas to help children learn to hear and say the initial sound in words, show an awareness of rhyme, distinguish different alphabet sounds and begin to form letters, linking the sounds to the names.

Alphabet riddles

What you need
Just the children.

What to do
Explain to the children that you are going to tell them some riddles and you would like them to work out the answers. Say that you will give them a clue to a word and that they must try to guess what the word is. Explain that you will tell them two things about the word; first the name of the letter that the word begins with, then you will give them a second clue.

Now tell the children the first riddle. Say, 'The person that I am thinking about begins with the sound 'a' and travels into space in a spaceship'. Remind them that the word that you want them to say begins with the sound 'a'. Ask the children if anyone knows what the word might be.

When the children have guessed the first word, say the following clues.
■ This person begins with the sound 'b'. He makes bread and cakes for us.
■ This person begins with the sound 'c' and works in a circus. He does funny things and makes us laugh.
■ This person begins with the sound 'd'. She wears a stethoscope and looks after us when we are ill.
■ This person begins with the sound 'e' and fixes electric wires.
■ This person begins with the sound 'f' and pours water on burning buildings to put the fire out.

When the children have answered all the riddles, list each occupation, saying the name of the first letter after each one. Ask the children if they notice anything about the order of the first letters.

Support and extension
Give the first syllables of the answers to the riddles to help younger children. Challenge older children to think up clues for different occupations using other letters of the alphabet.

Further idea
■ Play the game focussing on different categories of words, such as the names of fruits and vegetables or animals.

LEARNING OBJECTIVES
STEPPING STONE
Hear and say the initial sound in words.

EARLY LEARNING GOAL
Link sounds to letters, naming and sounding the letters of the alphabet.

GROUP SIZE
Any size.

HOME LINKS
Encourage parents and carers to play 'I spy' with their children. Ask them to give an additional clue as well as the sound of the letter. Have a 'letter of the week'. Invite the children to bring in items from home that begin with that letter sound to display.

'B' is for Bear

What you need
A teddy bear.

What to do
Introduce the teddy bear to the children. Explain that Bear is a special bear because he only likes things that begin with the same sound as his name. Ask the children to tell you what sound Bear's name begins with.

Now explain that you are going to say some pairs of words. Tell the children that you would like them to listen very carefully to the sound at the beginning of each word. Explain that you are going to say two things and you would like them to name which one Bear would choose. Remind them that their choice must start with the same sound as Bear.

Ask the children whether they think that Bear's favourite fruit would be apples or bananas, adding the question, 'Which word has the same sound at the beginning as Bear's name?'.

When the children have worked out the correct answer, go through the following questions in turn:

■ What is Bear's favourite toy: a bat and ball or a toy train?
■ What is Bear's favourite food: tinned tomatoes or baked beans?
■ What does Bear like to wear: pink pants or blue boots?
■ How does Bear like to travel: on a boat or in a car?
■ What is Bear's favourite nursery rhyme: Little Boy Blue or Simple Simon?

Support and extension
When asking younger children the questions, help them to say the first sound in Bear, and in each of the other words, before inviting them to make their choice. Rather than providing options for older children, use open-ended questions such as 'Which fruit would Bear like?'.

Further ideas
■ Invite the children to draw a picture of Bear with all his favourite things around him.
■ Encourage the children to add any other things beginning with a 'b' sound that they think he might like.
■ Ask the children to choose another character from the toy-box and to think of things that it would like that start with the same sound as the toy's name.

Hens in hats

What you need
Just the children.

What to do
Explain to the children that they are going to play a game with sounds. Start by asking if any of the children have ever seen animals wearing clothes. Point out that this would be very unusual and look very funny. Say, 'Well, I have never seen hens in hats, have you?'.

Tell the children to listen carefully to the two words, 'hens' and 'hats', and ask what they notice about the first sound in each of the words. Point out that both words start with the same sound.

Now explain that you are going to say an item of clothing and that you would like the children to think of an animal beginning with the same sound. When they have thought of one, ask them to put up their hand and say the sentence, for example, 'I have never seen cows in coats'.

Work through the following items of clothing to make up sentences such as, 'I have never seen pigs in pyjamas; …sheep in shoes; …ducks in dungarees; …worms in waistcoats; …slugs in slippers; …butterflies in boots; …turkeys in tights' and so on.

Support and extension
Encourage younger children by making an appropriate animal noise to help them to describe the animal. Ask older children to think of different animals to go with each item of clothing, or to think up other combinations of animals and clothes.

■■■■■■■■■■■■■■■■■■■■■■■■■■■■■■■■■■■

Further ideas
■ Instead of clothing, use the names of vehicles as the stimulus words, for example, van, lorry, train, bike, car, plane and so on, to produce sentences such as, 'I have never seen a bear on a bike'.

■ Use the children's names to make up alliterative sentences about things they would never wear or eat, such as 'Peter would never wear purple pyjamas'.

LEARNING OBJECTIVES
STEPPING STONE
Show awareness of rhyme and alliteration.

EARLY LEARNING GOAL
Hear and say initial and final sounds in words.

■■■■■■■■

GROUP SIZE
Any size.

■■■■■■■■

HOME LINKS
Suggest that parents and carers play a game with their children in which they name an animal. Their children should think of a food beginning with the same sound and put it into a sentence, for example, 'Ladybirds like lemonade'.

■■■■■■■■

Fish a picture

What you need
The photocopiable sheet on page 69; thin card; nine paper clips; short garden cane; string; magnet, bucket or waste-paper bin; pencils; paper.

Preparation
Photocopy the pictures on the photocopiable sheet on to thin card and cut them into nine individual pictures. Fix a paper clip to each picture. Make a 'fishing rod' by tying one end of a length of string to the garden cane and the other end to the magnet.

What to do
Place the pictures in the bucket and explain to the children that they are going to take turns to 'fish' the pictures out.

Give the fishing rod to the first child and show them how to dangle the magnet into the bucket to catch a picture. When they have caught one, ask them to show it to the other children. Encourage them to name the item in the picture. Then ask them what sound they can hear at the beginning of the word. Next, give each child a piece of paper and a pencil and invite them to write the letter that has been named.

Now let the children take turns to fish a picture from the bucket, following the same procedure each time, until the bucket is empty.

Support and extension
Help younger children to name each of the letters and write a model of the letter for them to copy. Ask older children if they can tell you which shape they write at the beginning of each letter.

Further ideas
■ Collect pictures from magazines that illustrate items beginning with letters from another letter formation group, such as 'r', 'n', 'm', 'h', and 'b', and use pictures in the same way as above.
■ Sprinkle some salt from a salt cellar over a baking tray to create large salt letters and practise the movements for a particular letter before using a pencil and paper.
■ Use plastic pockets and a wipe-clean pen to practise tracing over letter shapes in the correct way.

What's missing?

What you need
Strips of thin card, approximately 20cm x 6cm; marker pen; wooden or plastic letters.

Preparation
Write sequences of four letters from the alphabet on to the strips of card, omitting one letter and substituting a question mark instead, for example, 'a b ? d' and 'e ? g h'. Use a sequence of six letters on the last card to complete the alphabet.

What to do
Tell the children that they are going to try to help you find some missing letters. Show them the first card with the sequence from a to d. Explain that the beginning of the alphabet is written on the card, but that one letter is missing. Point out the question mark and say that this is where the missing letter should be.

Invite the children to say the first four letters of the alphabet. Then ask them to repeat these letters and to look carefully at the card as they do so. Ask them to tell you which letter is missing.

Now spread the wooden letters on the table and encourage the children to hunt through the letters to find the letter 'c'. Ask them to place the letter in the correct position on the card.

Move on to the next card and repeat the procedure, gradually building up the alphabet.

Support and extension
Tell younger children the letter sequence first and ask them to repeat it. Point to each letter as they say it. Give them just a few wooden letters to choose from for each card. Try using the cards out of alphabetical order with older children and encourage them to sort the cards into the correct order.

Further ideas
■ Make a second set of cards with different letters missing from the sequences.
■ Ask the children to listen very carefully as you say the alphabet out loud. Explain that you will stop suddenly and that they must call out the next letter.

Letter muncher

What you need
Five pieces of thin card (8cm²); marker pen; wooden or plastic letters.

Preparation
Write a word ending ('og', 'at', 'ig', 'ox', 'en') towards the right-hand side of each piece of card, leaving room for a wooden or plastic letter to be placed on the left-hand side.

What to do
Lay out the wooden or plastic letters ('d', 'c', 'p', 'h', 'f', 'r') on the table.

Give each child a word ending. Explain that the letters are the endings of the names of animals. Tell the children that the first letters of the words have been eaten by the 'letter muncher' and that you would like them to replace the correct letter at the beginning of the words.

Ask each child to sound out their two letters and to blend them together, saying the sound out loud. Then ask each child if they can think of an animal whose name ends in this way.

When all the children have named an appropriate animal, ask them to say the first sound in their animal's name. Invite them to check the letters on the table to see if they can find the letter that writes the sound that they need to make their animal words. (Be careful about where the children are positioned in relation to the letters, especially d and p.)

Encourage each child to put the correct letter on their card to complete their animal word. There will be one letter remaining as 'at' may be made into either 'cat' or 'rat'.

Support and extension
Read the word-endings to younger children. Invite older children to try other letters at the beginning of their word-endings to make new words.

Further ideas
■ Show cards with the first two letters of the animal names to the children and ask them to find the correct end letters.
■ Play 'Letter lotto'. Give each child a sheet of paper with two word-endings on it. Take one wooden letter at a time from a bag and see who can complete a word with it. The first person to complete both word wins.

Shuffles

What you need
Four pieces of thin card, approximately 10cm x 6cm; marker pen; scissors.

What to do
Tell the children that they are going to play a word game.

Explain that you will write the name of a different animal on each piece of card. Write the word 'bat' on the first piece of card. Pass it to a child and ask them to sound out the letters and read the word. Ask the other children to do the same with 'fox', 'dog' and 'pig'.

Now cut off the first letter from each word and place it in the middle of the table. As you do this, say, for example, 'I've cut the 'c' sound from cat. What does this leave us with?'

When all four initial letters have been cut from the words, tell the children that they you would like them to put each of the four letters on the table in front of the word-endings to see if they can make new words. Encourage them to move the letters around until each letter fits in front of a word-ending to build four new words that make sense. Point out that these new words will not be animal names.

Let the children move the initial letters around, sounding out any words or non-words that they make, until they finally build the words 'pat', 'box', 'fog' and 'dig'.

Support and extension
Help younger children to sound out words as they move the letters around. Let older children make lists of any new words that they make as they work towards the final four words.

Further ideas
■ Try different word-shuffle games such as 'run', 'gap', 'tin' and 'pat', with initial letters shuffled to make 'tap', 'gun', 'pin' and 'rat'.
■ Use the words 'pat', 'pin', 'rob' and 'rip', and ask the children to shuffle the last letters to make 'pan', 'rot', 'rib' and 'pip'.

Beginnings and endings

What you need

The photocopiable sheet on page 70; three sheets of thin A4 card; marker pen; scissors.

Preparation

Copy the photocopiable sheet on to a sheet of card and cut out the pictures. Make two baseboards by dividing the other two sheets of card into four and writing the words 'hen', 'mat', 'hat' and 'men' on one, and 'bug', 'rug', 'bat' and 'rat' on the other.

What to do

Give each child a baseboard. Show them the pictures and invite them to name each picture. Explain that four of the words are written on each of the boards. Shuffle the pictures and place them face down on the table.

Ask the first child to turn over a picture and look for the matching word on their baseboard. Encourage them to say the initial sound of the word and to check the beginning of their words for the appropriate letter. If they cannot find it, ask them to put the picture at the bottom of the pile.

If the child does find the words with the appropriate initial letter, encourage them to look at the word-endings carefully to see which one matches the picture. When they find the correct word-ending, invite them to place the picture on the word. Let the children take turns until one child has covered all of their words.

Support and extension

Help younger children to sound out the words on their baseboards before they begin. Point out to older children that they have more than one word with the same sound and the same ending on their board. Then let them play without drawing further attention to the detail of the words.

Further ideas

■ Write the words on to separate pieces of card rather than baseboards and use them with the pictures to play a game of 'Pairs'.
■ Give a group of children either one picture or one word card each and ask them to 'find their partner.' Encourage them to repeat the initial sound of their words or pictures to help them locate each other.

Check it!

What you need
The photocopiable sheet on page 71; sheet of thin A4 card; eight pieces of card, approximately 6cm x 4cm; marker pen; scissors.

Preparation
Copy the photocopiable sheet on to a sheet of thin card and cut out the pictures. Write the words 'pig', 'peg', 'cap', 'cup', 'leg', 'log', 'dig', 'dog' on to eight small pieces of card.

What to do
Explain to the children that they are going to be 'word detectives'. Place a pair of pictures in front of each child with a word below each picture. For two children, place the correct words below the pictures and for the other two children, place the word with the wrong middle sound below the pictures. For example, put the word 'cap' below the picture of the cup and the word 'cup' below the picture of the cap.

Ask the children to say what they see in their two pictures. Encourage them to tell you the sound that they can hear at the beginning, the end and in the middle of each word.

Now tell the children to look at the words below the pictures and to say whether they are the correct words for the pictures or not.

Support and extension
With younger children, present only one pair of pictures at a time. Use the pairs where the initial letter differs (pig/dig, leg/peg, dog/log) and let the children work together to decide whether the words are with the correct pictures. With older children, omit sounding out the picture names first and encourage them to look particularly carefully at the middle of the words.

Further ideas
■ Play oral games in which you tell the children that you will say two words and they must tell you if they begin with the same sound or not. Include some easily distinguishable initial sounds and more difficult pairs such as 'f'/'v', 'b'/ 'p' and 'd'/'t'.
■ Photocopy and enlarge a piece of newsprint and ask the children to hunt for words that begin with the same letter as their name.

LEARNING OBJECTIVES
STEPPING STONE
Understand the concept of a word.

EARLY LEARNING GOAL
Read a range of familiar and common words.

GROUP SIZE
Four children.

HOME LINKS
Ask parents and carers to play a game with their children thinking of as many words as possible beginning with the same sound.

Try this word

What you need
Pieces of thin card, approximately 6cm x 4cm; marker pen; paper; pencils.

Preparation
Make a word pack by writing simple some three-letter words on to pieces of card. Use phonically regular words such as 'cat', 'ham', 'dog', 'lot', 'pen', 'fun' and so on.

What to do
Place the pack of word cards face down on the table. Give each child a sheet of paper and a pencil and explain that they are going to play a word game. Say that one child will be the reader for each turn and the rest will be the writers.

Invite a child to start. Ask them to turn over the top card and to read the word, sounding out the letters, if necessary. Make sure that they say the word clearly so that the other children can hear it. Encourage the child to put the card face down on the table in front of them and to ask the others to try to write the word.

When they have finished, ask the child to turn the card over again and to say the names of the letters in the word, one by one. Encourage them to hold the card up so that the other children can check what they have written.

Now move around the group with each child taking a turn to be the 'reader'.

Support and extension
Sound out the words for younger children and ask them to blend the sounds for reading. Break the word down into sounds for spelling. Introduce a few words with initial blends for older children, such as 'slip', 'crab' and 'stop'.

Further idea
■ Make a display of objects with phonically regular names such as 'hat', 'bag', 'cup' and 'pen'. Say that you are thinking of one of the things and ask the children to write down their guess. Check who guessed correctly.
■ Place an object with a phonically regular name into a bag. Ask the children to try to guess what it is by feel and to write down their guess. Then check to see if they were correct.

Mathematical development

While taking part in the activities in this chapter, the children will be encouraged to use a range of mathematical language in play to describe different objects, say and use number names in order in familiar contexts and show an interest in talking about shapes, arrangements and simple patterns.

Big and little

What you need
An alphabet strip of lower-case letters.

What to do
Place the alphabet strip where it is clearly visible for all the children. Explain that all the letters that we need to make all the words in English are written on this alphabet. Tell them that there are 26 letters.

Now ask the children to look very carefully at the letters at the beginning of the alphabet while you say a rhyme. Point to each of the first four letters in turn as you say:

> First comes little letter 'a'
> then big letter 'b'
> then little letter 'c'
> and big letter 'd'.

Invite the children to remind you which letters you said were big and which were little. Draw their attention to the fact that the letters are not the same height, and that it is important to remember this when writing.

Encourage the children to look along the alphabet strip to find other letters that are little and others that are big.

Support and extension
Allow younger children to point to the big and little letters rather than naming them. Write the first four letters of the alphabet only for older children and ask them to tell you each following letter in turn, saying whether it is a big or a little letter.

■■■

Further ideas
■ Place an alphabet strip of capital letters (exactly the same height as each other) beneath the lower-case letters. Talk about the special use of these letters for names and places. Then ask the children if they notice anything about the height of these letters.
■ Provide the children with pieces of card as measures, one cut to the height of the 'little' letters and the other to the height of the 'big' letters. Invite the children to use these cards to check along the alphabet line to decide whether letters are big or little.

Letter towers

What you need
An alphabet strip showing capital letters large enough that Duplo bricks can be placed in front of each letter; Duplo bricks or similar; paper; coloured pencils; Blu-Tack.

What to do
Tell the children that they are going to find out which letter of the alphabet starts more of their names than any other letter. Show them the alphabet strip and ask each child to pick up a Duplo brick.

Explain that each child is going to place a brick in front of the letter that starts his or her name. Tell them that if there is more than one person whose name begins with any letter, to place the bricks on top of each other. Say that they will quickly be able to see which 'letter tower' is higher than the others. This will tell them which letter starts more names than any other.

Let the children place their bricks in turn. During the activity, talk about which tower is higher or lower than the rest. When all the bricks are in place, write letters on to small pieces of paper and attach them to the relevant towers with Blu-Tack. Now ask the children to place the highest tower at the left of the table and to measure the other towers against each other. Encourage them to arrange the towers in order of decreasing height. Say, for example, 'Can you find me a tower which is a bit smaller than the "s" tower?'.

Support and extension
Help younger children to place their bricks by the correct letter and to move the towers into height order. Let older children transfer their findings on to large squared-paper to make a simple bar chart.

Further ideas
■ You could use the children's second names instead of their first names and compare their findings.
■ Dismantle the towers and count the number of bricks in each one. Encourage the children to record their findings by writing a given letter and drawing the correct number of children beside it.

One worm wiggled

What you need
Just the children.

Preparation
Familiarise yourself with the rhyme below.

What to do
Tell the children that you are going to read a number rhyme to them and then you would like them to say it with you.

Read the following rhyme, holding up the appropriate number of fingers for each line:

> *One worm wiggled its way along the ground.*
> *Two tired tortoises slept without a sound.*
> *Three thrushes sang a song until their throats were dry.*
> *Four frogs flicked their tongues and caught a juicy fly.*
> *Five furry foxes followed fluffy hen.*
> *She got away and they went back hungry to their den.*

Invite the children to join in with you on the second reading.

Now say that you would like them to listen very carefully to some words from the first line of the rhyme. Say the words 'one', 'worm', 'wiggled' and 'way', and ask the children if they notice anything about the sound at the beginning of all these words. (Point out that the words begin with the same sound.)

Now work through the next four lines of the rhyme, picking out the alliterative words and asking what the children notice about the initial sound.

Support and extension
Help younger children by emphasising the initial sounds of the words. Give older children the number word and ask them to tell you which other words in the line begin with the same sound.

Further ideas
■ Put actions to the rhyme – wiggle a forefinger for line one; put hands to side of head for line two; put heads back and stretch throats for line three; flick out tongues for line four; 'walk' fingers for line five; hang heads and look sad for the last two lines.
■ Say a number and ask the children to think of as many words as possible beginning with the same sound.
■ Ask the children to paint pictures to make a number frieze. Write the number word and the alliterating words beneath each picture.

LEARNING OBJECTIVES

STEPPING STONE
Enjoy joining in with number rhymes and songs.

EARLY LEARNING GOAL
Say and use number names in order in familiar contexts.

GROUP SIZE
Any size.

HOME LINKS
Send the rhyme home and encourage parents and carers to help their children learn it.

Letter number nine

What you need
An alphabet strip of lower-case letters.

What to do
Tell the children that you are going to ask them some questions about the alphabet. Show them the alphabet strip and recite the alphabet together, pointing to each letter as it is named.

Now ask the children if they know how many letters there are in the alphabet. Suggest that you count the letters in the alphabet together to find out. Again, point to each letter as the children count.

Explain to the children that, when you say a number, you would like them to count along the alphabet strip and to tell you which letter they land on when they reach that number. Make sure that they understand that they must start counting at the letter 'a'. Now say a low number, such as 'three'. Count with the children to reach letter 'c' and say, '"c" is letter number three in the alphabet. Can you tell me which letter is number five in the alphabet?'.

Continue in this way with the children until you reach the end of the alphabet strip.

Support and extension
Use only lower numbers with younger children and count along to the letter with them. Challenge older children to tell you the letter that you want without them looking at the alphabet line.

Further ideas
■ Play the game by naming a letter and ask the children to tell which number this letter is in the alphabet.
■ Use the children's own names to play similar games. Ask, for example, 'Which letter is number three in your name?'.
■ In a robotic voice, sound out simple three-letter words and ask the children which sound was number one, two or three in the word.
■ Tell the children a number, then ask them to count down the tabs on an address or telephone number book, and to tell you the letter. Show them how you would look up addresses or phone numbers using such an index.

Whose name?

What you need
Paper; pencils; sheet of A1 card or paper; marker pen.

Preparation
Using the marker pen, write the numerals 1–10 down the left-hand side of the sheet of A1 card.

What to do
Choose two of the children's names, one short and one long, to write on a piece of paper. Hold this up to show the children and point out that one name is much longer than the other because it has more letters in it.

Explain to the children that they are going to try to find out whose name has the most letters in it.

Give each child a piece of paper and a pencil and ask them to write down their name. Help them if necessary. Ask each child in turn to give you their piece of paper and hold it up so that everyone can see the name. Point to each letter in turn and ask the children to count with you as you point. When the letters have been counted, write the name on the sheet of card next to the appropriate numeral. Say the name and state the number of letters, before moving on to the next child's name.

When all the names have been written on the chart, read the information back to the children, saying, 'Sam and Ben have three letters in their name,' and so on. Then ask the children, 'Who has the most letters in their name? Who has the least?'.

Support and extension
Work in small groups with younger children. Write their names for them and then guide their fingers to helps them count the letters. Ask older children to write their own names next to the correct numeral on the chart.

Further idea
■ Count the letters in the names of nursery rhyme characters or favourite characters from fairy-tales.

Put it in order

What you need
The photocopiable sheet on page 72; ruler; pen; thin A4 card.

Preparation
Make four copies of the photocopiable sheet on to thin card and cut out the pictures. Divide the back of each picture into four equal vertical strips. Then write the letters 'a', 'b', 'c' and 'd', one in each section, from right to left, on the first picture, and 'e', 'f', 'g', 'h' on the second picture. Cut the pictures into four strips.

What to do
Give each child the four sections of the first picture, reverse side up, to show the letters. Lay the letters out in front of the child in the wrong sequence.

Invite the children to say the alphabet with you. When you have finished, point to the four letters and say, 'You have the first four letters of the alphabet. Can you put them in the correct order?'. Show the children how to place the first letter on the left. As they work, use words such as 'first' and 'second', 'before' and 'after', to talk about the letter order.

When the letters are in the correct order, invite the children to turn the strips over, one by one, and to push them together. Explain that if the letters are in the correct order, they should have a picture of a crocodile.

Now repeat the procedure with the second picture, asking the children to put these letters in the correct order. Remind them how to check if they have made a picture of an elephant.

Support and extension
Let younger children work together to decide the correct order of the letters. Model the arrangement for the children to copy. Encourage older children to try to arrange the letters without saying the alphabet first.

Further ideas
■ Cut out pictures from magazines and stick them on to pieces of card to create pictures to practise other four-letter sequences taken from the middle and the end of the alphabet.
■ Play oral alphabet games. Ask the children which letter comes after 'g', before 't' and so on.

Spot the shape

What you need
The photocopiable sheet on page 73; red and blue coloured pencils.

Preparation
Copy the photocopiable sheet for each child.

What to do
Show the children the group of letters on the top half of their photocopiable sheets. Explain that one letter in the group has been printed many more times than any other. Tell them that it is the letter 't'.

Give each child a red coloured pencil and ask them to look carefully along each of the rows of letters. Say that you would like them to draw a red circle around the letter 't' each time that they find it. Explain that there might be more than one letter 't' in a row.

When the children have looked through the rows and circled the letters, check that they have not missed any.

Now ask the children to look carefully at the letters with the red circles around them. Tell them that they have been arranged to make a certain shape. Ask them if they can tell you what the shape is.

Say the word 'triangle' emphasising the initial sound. Ask the children what sound they can hear at the beginning of 'triangle' and which letter writes that sound. Show them that the letter 't' at the beginning of the word 'triangle' has been used to make the triangle shape.

Repeat the activity with the group of letters at the bottom of the photocopiable sheet. This time ask the children to look for the letter 'r' and to circle it using a blue coloured pencil. The circled letters will create a square.

Support and extension
You can provide younger children with a written model of the letters that they are looking for. Ask older children why they think the letters have been arranged as they have, without drawing their attention to the initial sound of the shapes first.

■ ■

Further idea
■ Write the same letter repeatedly and randomly on a page. Write other letters on the page, interspersed with the repeated letter. Ask the children to hunt out the repeated letter.

LEARNING
OBJECTIVES
STEPPING STONE
Show interest by
talking about shapes
or arrangements.

**EARLY LEARNING
GOAL**
Talk about, recognise
and recreate simple
patterns.

GROUP SIZE
Four children.

HOME LINKS
Suggest that parents
and carers help their
children to recognise
one letter from
another by playing
a game in which
they write a row
of repeated letters,
with only one letter
different and ask
their child to find the
'odd letter out'.

Jigsaw letters

What you need
Three pieces of thin card (8cm²); marker pen; ruler; pencil; three pairs of child-safety scissors.

Preparation
Write a different lower-case letter on each of the pieces of card, spanning the centre of the card.

What to do
Give each child a piece of card and ask them to look carefully at the letter on their card.

Now ask each child, in turn, some questions about the shape of their letter. Does any part of the letter have a curved shape, or does it have a curly tail? Is any side of the letter straight? Encourage the children to trace around their letter shape with their forefinger, sounding and naming the letter.

Next, draw a pencil line across each card, through the middle of the letter. Tell the children that they are going to make puzzles. Give each child a pair of scissors and invite them to cut the card in half along the pencil line. Shuffle the six pieces of card on the table. Ask the children to find the two parts of their letter and to put them back together again. As the children work, remind them of what they told you about the shape of their letter.

Support and extension
Sound out and name the letters for younger children and help them with cutting, if necessary. Turn the six pieces of card face down for older children and play a pairs game to find the two matching letter pieces.

Further ideas
■ Stick pictures on the back of the cards of an object beginning with the relevant letter. When the children have matched the letter, invite them to turn the card over to see which object they have matched as well. Draw their attention to the initial sound.
■ Write the alphabet on to long strips of thin card. Make different cuts between the letters to help the children arrange them into the correct alphabetical order.

LEARNING OBJECTIVES
STEPPING STONE
Begin to talk about the shapes of everyday objects.

EARLY LEARNING GOAL
Talk about, recognise and recreate simple patterns.

GROUP SIZE
Three children.

HOME LINKS
Encourage parents and carers to write lower-case letters on pieces of paper. Ask them to cover one half of the letter and invite their children to look at the remaining shape and to guess which letter it is.

In the box, on the box

What you need
Two lidded boxes of different colours; ten small-world play items such as toy cars or farm animals; two pieces of A5 card; marker pen.

Preparation
Write the word 'in' in large lower-case letters on one piece of card and the word 'on' on the second piece of card.

What to do
Explain to the children that you are going to ask them to place each of the play items in turn, either in one of the boxes or on it. Say that you will hold up a card to tell them where you would like the play item to be placed.

Now show the children the two cards. Point to the 'in' card and encourage them to look very carefully at the word that is written on it. Ask, 'Can you tell me the sound that the first letter in this word makes?'. Then ask whether they think the word says 'in' or 'on'. Tell the children that if you hold this word card up, they should put their play item in the box. Repeat this procedure with the other card.

Then hold up one of the positional word cards and tell the first child what to do, saying, for example, 'Sally, please put the blue car ___ the red box'.

Continue in this way until all the items have been placed either in or on one of the boxes.

Support and extension
Help to familiarise younger children with the words by consistently using one box for objects to be placed inside and the other for them to be placed on top. Ask older children to take turns giving the instructions and holding up the cards.

■■■■■■■■■■■■■■■■■■■■■■■■■■■■■■■■■■■■

Further ideas
■ Add cards with the words 'next to' and 'behind'. Focus the children's attention on the initial letters and sounds to help them use these cards and understand where they should place the items.
■ Ask the children to look at the instruction card, then place themselves, rather than toys, 'in', 'on', 'next to' or 'behind' an object in the room.

LEARNING OBJECTIVES
STEPPING STONE
Observe and use positional language.

EARLY LEARNING GOAL
Use everyday words to describe position.

GROUP SIZE
Five children.

HOME LINKS
Ask parents and carers to play a 'hunt the thimble' game and to use similar cards as clues to tell their children whether they should look 'in', 'on', 'next to' or 'behind' things for the hidden object.

Word sums

What you need
A check-list of initial sounds to place in front of 'it' to make words.

What to do
Tell the children that they are going to do some sums. Say that these are not the sort of sums where they add numbers together, but they are going to add sounds together to make words.

Now say, 'I am going to start with the sound "s" (say the sound without an 'uh' sound after it), then I am going to add "it" to that sound'. Say, 's–it' (with a one-second pause after the initial sound), then say the word, 'sit'. Ask the children if they could actually hear that you made the word 'sit'.

Tell the children that it is their turn now. Explain that you would like them to add the two sounds that you say together and to tell you the word that they have made.

Say, 'f–it' (as it is described above). Ask them to repeat what you have said and ask which word this makes.

Use different initial sounds from your list. Make sure that you always say the initial sound cleanly, without an obvious 'uh' sound included in it.

Support and extension
Help younger children by blending the initial sound with 'it' for them and just asking them to repeat the word that you have made. Ask older children to tell you the word without repeating what you have said first.

Further ideas
■ Blend initial sounds with endings such as 'in' and 'am' instead of 'it'.
■ Start with three-letter words such as sit, pit, bit, lit, kit and so on, and ask the children to take away the sound at the beginning and tell you which word is left.
■ Give the children three-letter words and ask them to add an extra sound on to the end to make a new word, for example, 'ten + t'; 'pin + k'; 'win + d'; 'pan + t'; 'sun + k'; 'men + d'; 'den + t'; 'bun + k'; 'ban + d'.

Knowledge and understanding of the world

This chapter suggests ideas to enable children to investigate everyday objects, showing curiosity and asking questions about the natural world, while beginning to learn about their own cultures and beliefs, and other people's.

Taste a letter

What you need
Small amounts of bread, butter, banana, baked beans and cooked beetroot; five saucers; five teaspoons; empty cereal boxes.

Preparation
Check for any food allergies and dietary requirements. Place a small amount of each food on to different saucers. Make a screen along the middle of a table of folded pieces of card from cereal boxes.

What to do
Invite the children to a 'taste testing' session. Explain that you are going to ask them to close their eyes and taste something from a spoon, and you would like them to guess what it is.

Seat the children on one side of a table with the foods screened off by the pieces of card. Ask each child, in turn, to close their eyes and then give them a small amount of one type of food to taste. Give them something different and encourage them to guess what the food is. If necessary, prompt the children until they name the correct food. Now ask a child to think about the sound at the beginning of their food word and to tell you what it is.

Ask the children the name of the food that they tasted, to say if the sound at the beginning of each food was the same and to say what the letter was.

Support and extension
Tell younger children the initial sound to help them guess the foods. Check afterwards that they noticed that all of the foods started with the same sound. Invite older children to guess the foods that they have tasted and then list them. Ask them if they notice anything about all the words without mentioning the initial sound.

Further ideas
■ Try other groups of food with different initial sounds, such as cake, carrot, coconut, or pear, peaches, pineapple (tinned fruit can be used) and pickle.
■ Ask the children to draw the food that they tasted. Let them cut out the pictures and stick them to a paper plate to create 'alphabet meals'.

Birthday box

What you need
A cardboard box; card; balloon; birthday card; sticky tape; safety pin; felt-tipped pens.

Preparation
Make a simple birthday badge using the card, sticky tape, felt-tipped pens and safety pin. Place this, along with the balloon and the birthday card, inside the box ready for the activity.

What to do
Show the children the special 'birthday box'. Ask if they notice anything about the sounds at the beginning of the words 'birthday' and 'box'. Point out that they begin with the same sound.

Remove the balloon from the box. Ask the children whether the sound at the beginning of this word is the same as the sound at the start of 'birthday' and 'box'. Now take out the badge, again asking the children about the initial sound. Finally, remove the birthday card. Remind the children that all the things from the box start with the same sound.

Explain that now you are going to say the sound at the beginning of the name of someone whose birthday it is today. Alternatively, explain that the child with a birthday also has a name beginning with a 'b' sound. Ask the children to guess whose birthday it is. When they have guessed, invite the birthday child to talk about how they are going to celebrate their birthday.

Support and extension
Tell younger children that all the items in the box begin with the same sound and extend that sound as you name the objects. Encourage older children to show you how to write the letter 'b'.

Further ideas
■ Encourage the children to think of birthday presents that they could give to the birthday child that begin with a 'b' sound, or food that they could eat at a birthday party beginning with that same sound.
■ Take a cracker, candle, Christmas cake and a Christmas card out of a carrier bag and discuss the initial sounds. Lead into a discussion about Christmas, then other important festivals such as Hanukkah and Divali.

Who's who?

What you need
Small-world farm animals, farm buildings and machinery.

Preparation
Decide on names for each animal and make a note of them. Choose names that alliterate with each animal, for example, 'Henry the horse', 'Percy the pig' or 'Derek the duck'.

What to do
Show the children the animals and explain that they are going to make a farm. Say that you are going to discuss the animals one at a time. Tell the children that you will think of an animal to give them and that you would like them to guess which animal it is. Explain that you are going to give them a clue by telling them the animal's name, for example, 'The animal that I am thinking of starts with the same sound as his name – Henry the ..... Which animal am I going to give you that starts with the same sound as the name Henry?'.

If there you find there is more than one possibility for an animal, for example, a duck or dog, give the children an additional clue, such as, 'This animal lives in a pond'.

As the children guess each animal, discuss with them where that animal would be kept on the farm and the role that it would play. You could say as an example, 'Farmers will keep sheep because they give us wool to make clothes'.

Support and extension
Give younger children the relevant initial sound after you have given the name, rather than letting them extract this from the name themselves. Ask older children to tell you the sound of the letter at the beginning of an animal word. Offer to give them the animal if they can think of a name for it that begins with the same sound as the animal word.

LEARNING OBJECTIVES
STEPPING STONE
Comment and ask questions about the natural world.

EARLY LEARNING GOAL
Observe, find out about and identify features in the natural world.

GROUP SIZE
Four children.

HOME LINKS
Ask parents and carers to explore with their children whether they have given their toys names with the same initial sound as the toy word, for example, 'Rachel the rabbit'.

Further ideas
■ Invite the children to think up alliterative names for small-world play vehicles, such as diggers and road-rollers.
■ Encourage the children to think up imaginary alliterative names for a range of animals that tell you something about the way that they move or look, for example, 'Hoppity Hare' or 'Freckly Frog'.

Animal alphabet

What you need
An alphabet line; the photocopiable sheets on pages 74 to 77 (the names of each of the animals can be found in the 'Alphabet zoo' rhyme on page 42); thin card; children's picture alphabet book (optional).

Preparation
Copy the photocopiable sheets on to thin card. Familiarise yourself with the animal names in the 'Alphabet zoo' rhyme.

What to do
Invite the children to recite the alphabet. Lay out the pictures and explain that they are going to build an animal alphabet.

Point to the letter 'a' on the alphabet line and name it. Ask the children if they can tell you the sound that this letter writes. Now ask them to suggest animal names that begin with this sound. If they suggest 'alligator', say, 'That's the one we are going to look for'. Otherwise, say, 'Well done, but we need to look for an alligator'. Ask them to find the alligator picture.

When they have found the alligator, discuss the animal's appearance, and where it is found in the natural world. Talk about how easy or difficult it was to think of animals beginning with particular letters. Point out that some letters, such as 'y', do not come at the beginning of many words. If necessary, use the picture alphabet book to help the children.

Work through the alphabet, placing each animal picture beneath the appropriate initial letter.

Support and extension
Give the sound of the letter to younger children and describe the animal to help them find the correct picture. Let older children pick up the pictures in any order and try to match them to the correct initial letter, building up the alphabet in this way. As they pick up pictures, ask if this animal will come near the beginning, middle or end of the animal alphabet.

Further ideas
■ Invite the children to choose a favourite animal. Look through books together to try to find out more information about it.
■ Ask the children to look at the animal alphabet and count how many birds there are, how many sea creatures there are, how many animals with two legs there are (and so on).

10-MINUTE IDEAS: Alphabet fun

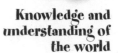
Look at letters

What you need
A set of wooden letters.

Preparation
Select the following wooden letters from the set: 'a', 'c', 'd', 'e', 'g', 'h', 'o' and 'q'.

What to do
Lay out the letters in alphabetical order on a table, explaining to the children that they are going to look very carefully at the letters to find one that is different from the rest.

Lift the letter 'c' from the sequence and trace your finger round it, saying, 'Look at the curly shape of this letter. Most of the other letters on the table have the same curly shape in them'.

Now lay the letter 'c' on top of the letter 'a'. Say, 'Can you see how the letter "c" fits exactly on top of this part of the letter "a"? That's because the letter "a" has the same curly shape in it'.

Invite the children to look at the remaining letters and to try to place the letter 'c' on top of each letter to see if it fits exactly on any part. Ask which letter is the odd one out.

Support and extension
Encourage younger children to trace around the letter 'c' with their finger, and then around each of the other letters to see if they can feel the 'c' shape, before placing the letter 'c' on top. With older children, omit the letters 'e' and 'q' from the sequence and challenge them to try all the other letters in the alphabet to find two more which share the same shape as the letter 'c'.

Further ideas
■ Carry out an activity using the letters 'b', 'h', 'm', 'n', 'p', 'r' and 't'. This time, use the letter 'r' as the cue shape, referring to the down, up and over movement that you make as you trace around the letter.

■ Using self-adhesive velour, trace around wooden letters and stick an alphabet sequence on to a large piece of card. Make a second set of letters on pieces of clear acetate. Let the children place the acetate on to the card to find the matching partner for each letter.

Alphabet zoo

What you need

An alphabet line; the photocopiable sheets on pages 74 to 77; thin card.

Preparation

Copy the photocopiable sheets on to thin card. If you are working with a larger group, you may wish to enlarge them.

What to do

Read the following rhyme to the children:

> *Alligator, bear, crocodile, dog,*
> *great big elephant and freckled frog,*
> *goat, hippopotamus, iguana, too,*
> *all live together in the alphabet zoo.*
> *Jaguar, kangaroo and lion, too,*
> *all live together in the alphabet zoo.*
> *Monkey, newt and ostrich, too,*
> *all live together in the alphabet zoo.*
> *Panda, quail and rabbit, too,*
> *all live together in the alphabet zoo.*
> *Snake and tiger, umbrella bird too,*
> *all live together in the alphabet zoo.*
> *Vole, whale, fox, yak and zebra, too,*
> *all live together in the alphabet zoo.*

Read the rhyme a few lines at a time, and ask the children to listen to the names of each animal very carefully. After the first four lines, name each animal in turn, and ask them which sound they can hear at the beginning of that name. Invite the children to tell you the name of the letter that writes that sound, pointing to the alphabet line.

Ask the children whether they have heard of each animal. Encourage them to describe the animal and to suggest where it would live if it were not in the 'animal zoo'. Show the picture of each animal as it is discussed.

Support and extension

With younger children, name the initial letters as you work along the alphabet line. Omit the alphabet line with older children and ask them if they notice anything about the order in which the animals are named.

Further ideas

■ Read the alphabet rhyme again, encouraging the children to join in with the repeated refrain.
■ Invite the children to paint or draw different animals and create a frieze with the animals displayed in alphabetical order.

Magic letters

What you need
Paper; paint mixed to a watery consistency; paintbrushes; aprons; white candle or white wax crayon.

Preparation
Using the white candle or wax crayon, write a large, lower-case letter on a piece of paper for each child.

What to do
Give each child a sheet of paper and tell them that you have written a secret letter on each sheet. Explain that you would like them to paint over the paper with the paint to make the letter appear. Invite the children to start painting at the bottom of the paper, and say that you would like them to guess what their particular letter might be, as soon as it begins to appear. Talk about things such as tails on letters, straight lines or curly shapes.

As the letters begin to emerge, draw each child's attention to the shape that they can see and discuss which letters this shape could belong to. Talk about how the paint is not sticking to some parts of the paper.

When the full letters are visible and the children have guessed their letter correctly, explain to them how you wrote them in candle wax or wax crayon. Let them feel the waxy surface and ask them why they think the paint did not stick on the parts of the paper on which you had written with wax.

Support and extension
Help younger children by suggesting, as their letter emerges, several letters that it could be, mentioning, for example, that this curly shape could be part of a letter 'c' or an 'a' or a 'g'. Do not tell older children what you used to write the letters and invite them to make suggestions of what it could have been.

Further ideas
■ Let the children create other magic letters for each other to reveal.
■ Provide a variety of different surfaces for the children to paint letters and explore which surfaces the paint will stick to, such as plastic cut from white carrier bags, kitchen towel, baking trays and a range of different papers.

LEARNING OBJECTIVES
STEPPING STONE
Talk about what is seen and what is happening.

EARLY LEARNING GOAL
Ask questions about why things happen and how things work.

GROUP SIZE
Four children.

HOME LINKS
Let the children make a wax-resist picture to take home for their parents or carers. Help them to write the recipient's name in white wax crayon before inviting the children to paint over the design.

From a to z

What you need
A computer or typewriter.

Preparation
If you are using a computer, open a word-processing file. Select a font such as Century Gothic, which has a cursive 'a' and 'g'.

What to do
Invite the children to recite the alphabet for you. Ask them which letter comes at the beginning of the alphabet and which letter comes right at the end.

Now ask the children to look at the computer or typewriter. Point to the first letter on the left in the top row of letters ('q'). Say, 'Remind me which letter comes at the beginning of the alphabet. Is it this letter here?'. Ask the children which letter comes after 'a' and then draw their attention to the second letter along on the first row of keyboard letters ('w'). Tell them to look carefully along the rows of letters to see if these are in the same order as the alphabet.

Explain to the children that some letters in the alphabet are used more often in words than others. Talk about the letters being arranged on the keyboard to make it easier to type in the letters that are used most often.

Ask the children to try to type the alphabet in order as far as they know it. As they do this, point out that there are two points in the alphabet where the order is the same on the keyboard ('j k l' and 'o p').

Support and extension
Provide an alphabet line for younger children to help them remember the order as they type. Assist them with finding the letters, explaining that keyboards always show capitals. Let older children tell you any other letter sequences from the alphabet that they discover to be in the same order on the keyboard.

Further ideas
■ Invite the children to type their names. Show them how to use the 'CAP' key to make the first letter a capital. If they are working on a computer, help them to change their name into different fonts and print out their favourite.
■ Encourage the children to explore books that use alphabetical order, such as dictionaries, telephone directories and address books.

Pass the bag

What you need
A set of wooden letters; opaque bag; tape recorder or CD player; music tape or CD.

Preparation
Place the wooden letters in the bag.

What to do
Invite the children to sit in a circle. Explain that you are going to give them a bag full of letters to pass around while music plays. Say that they should pass the bag around until the music stops.

Explain that the person that is holding the bag when the music stops should put their hand inside and hold one of the letters. Stress to them that they must not look inside the bag to see what the letter is, they should just feel it. Say that they can use both hands if they want to.

Start the music and encouraging the children to pass the bag around the circle. Then stop the music, and invite the child that is holding the bag to feel a letter. Ask the child to guess what the letter is and to think of something that begins with this letter. After the child has named something, ask them to pull the letter from the bag and check if their guess was correct. Start the music and play again.

Support and extension
Help younger children to feel the letter and talk about its shape. Encourage them to remove the letter from the bag, check their guess and make sure that they know the sound of the letter before they name an object. Ask older children to give two words beginning with the letter from the bag.

■■■

Further ideas
■ As the children remove letters from the bag, ask them to place them in a line, in alphabetical order, in the middle of the circle. Ask, 'Will this letter go near the beginning, middle or end of the alphabet?'.
■ When the children have picked a letter, ask them to look around the circle to find someone whose name begins with that letter.

LEARNING OBJECTIVES
STEPPING STONE
Show curiosity, observe and manipulate objects.

EARLY LEARNING GOAL
Investigate objects and materials by using all of their senses as appropriate.

■■■■■■■■■■

GROUP SIZE
Any size.
■■■■■■■■■■

HOME LINKS
Explain the game to parents and carers and suggest that they play a version of it with their children. They can omit the music and just take turns to feel a letter in the bag and name a word.
■■■■■■■■■

Easy or not?

What you need
Pieces of different materials such as paper (white and coloured), card, plastic, fabric, clay or Plasticine; a pencil for each child; kitchen roll.

Preparation
Sort a selection of materials, including a rolled-out square of clay or Plasticine, for each child.

What to do
Invite the children to write the initial letter of their name on a piece of paper. As they are writing, ask them to think about how easy it is to slide the pencil over the paper so that it makes a mark.

Now suggest to the children that they try to write the same letter on another piece of material that they have. Use each piece of material in turn and ask the children questions such as, 'How easy is it to make a mark?'; Do you need to press hard to make a mark?'; 'Is there a mark left at all?'; 'Does the material remain still as you work?' and 'How does the material feel?'. Clean the pencils with the kitchen roll after writing in the clay.

Invite the children to group together materials that were easy or difficult to write on and ask if they can think of anything that these materials have in common.

Support and extension
Encourage all attempts at writing from younger children and prompt them with questions such as, 'Are all the materials that were easy to write on smooth materials?'. Ask older children to predict which materials will be more difficult before they start to write and to make suggestions as to why this is.

Further ideas
■ Invite the children to experiment with different writing implements on the materials, such as felt-tipped pens and wax crayons, or to paint letters and see if this makes a difference.
■ Make clay tiles and encourage the children to decorate them with repeated engravings of their initials.
■ Experiment with different writing implements on blotting paper to see which leaves the clearest mark.

Physical development

The activities in this chapter encourage children to show an awareness of space while moving with confidence, control, co-ordination and safety, as well as beginning to use descriptive language for the shape or size of solids, and handle tools, objects and malleable materials with increasing control.

Acrobat Annie

What you need
Just the children.

What to do
Tell the children that you are going to read them a poem about some clever children who can move in different ways.

> Acrobat Annie, as everyone knows,
> can bend over easily and touch her toes.
> Bouncy Ben can jump up so high,
> you think he will disappear into the sky.
> Curly Catherine can curl up so small,
> you have to look hard to see Catherine at all.
> Dancing Dorothy twirls round and round,
> until she gets dizzy and falls to the ground.

Now tell the children to listen carefully to each of the names in the poem. Ask why they think that 'Bouncy Ben' was called 'Bouncy'. Do they notice anything about the sounds at the beginning of 'Bouncy' and 'Ben'?

Invite the children to do the same things as the children in the poem. Say that you are going to read the poem again and that you would like them to stand up and put the actions to it. Before you start, make sure that the children have plenty of space around them to move freely.

Support and extension
Demonstrate the actions for younger children before you re-read the poem. Invite older children to join in with the actions and say the rhyme with you.

Further ideas
■ Ask if the children can think of any words that have the same first sound as their name that describe something that they can do, then invite them to demonstrate the actions.
■ Give the children an action word, such as 'lively', and encourage them to think of another person's name to go with it that begins with the same sound. Then ask them to move like the person.
■ Share books that have alliterative titles reflecting the behaviour of the main character, such as 'Fearsome Fritz'.

LEARNING OBJECTIVES
STEPPING STONE
Respond to rhythm, music and story by means of gesture and movement.

EARLY LEARNING GOAL
Move with confidence, imagination and in safety.

GROUP SIZE
Any size.

HOME LINKS
Send home a copy of the poem and encourage parents and carers to help their children learn it.

Body letters

What you need
Six sheets of thin card; marker pen; large space.

Preparation
Write the letters 'c', 'o', 's', 'r', 'n' and 'u' in large lower case, one on each of the pieces of card.

What to do
Explain to the children that they are going to make some letter shapes by using their bodies. Ask them to spread out and make sure that they have plenty of space around them.

Hold up the letter 'c' card. Ask the children if they know the sound and then the name of this letter. Trace your finger around the 'c' and talk about the way that it curls around. Now ask the children to lie on the floor and curl their body into a 'c' shape. If necessary, walk around and help the children make the correct shape.

Next, show the children the letter 'o'. As you trace around it, point out to them that the shape starts like the letter 'c', but keeps on going and joins the beginning of the letter again. Encourage the children to make this shape with their body.

Continue through the letters in this way. Show the curling shape at the top of the letter 's' and point out that this letter then curls back the other way. Draw the children's attention to the similar shape at the beginning of the letters 'r' and 'n'. Talk about the similarity between the letters 'n' and 'u' and stress the importance of making sure that they are the correct way up.

Support and extension
Demonstrate to younger children the body shapes that you would like them to make. Ask older children to think of other letter shapes that they could make. If necessary, let them work with a partner.

Further ideas
■ Invite the children to work in pairs to form the letters 'h', 'b', 'p', 'm', 'w' and 'k'. Draw their attention to the similar straight lines and curves in 'h', 'b' and 'p'. Emphasise that 'm' and 'w' must be formed the correct way up, so that they are not confused.
■ Let the children bend pipe-cleaners into letter shapes. Use attractively coloured or glittery pipe-cleaners to make special initials to stick on to the front of a greetings card.

Letters in the air

What you need
Just the children.

What to do
Explain to the children that they are going to practise making letters shapes in the air. Tell them that you would like them to make each letter with both of their hands and that they are going to see which hand feels more comfortable for them.

Stand with your back to the children so that they can copy you exactly. Look over your shoulder to speak to them as you demonstrate. Start with the letter 'c', using your right arm and hand. Say, 'I would like you to make a big letter "c", using your right hand. We start at the top and come around in a big curve towards our body and then away from it again. Now try it with your left hand. With this hand, we start at the top, the same as before, but we make a big curve away from our body and then come back in towards it again'. Ask each child which hand felt more comfortable.

Now try further letters, building on the movement needed for the letter 'c'. Practise through 'o', 'a', 'd', 'g' and 'q', all of which have the same initial shape as 'c'. Then try the letter 's', which has the same movement abbreviated at the beginning. Follow this with the letter 'e' and tell the children that they must make an extra movement at the beginning before making the same curved movement, as for the letter 'c'.

At the end, ask the children which hand they felt it would be easier for them to use to write.

Support and extension
Help younger children by guiding their arms for them. With older children, work on the letter 'c', and then ask if they can think of other letters that they would begin with the same movement.

Further ideas
■ Work on a second letter formation group with similar initial movement patterns, for example 'r', 'n', 'm', 'h', 'b' and 'p'.
■ Practise large letter shapes by aiming a water pistol at an outside wall.

LEARNING OBJECTIVES
STEPPING STONE
Show a clear and consistent preference for the left or right hand.

EARLY LEARNING GOAL
Show awareness of space, of themselves and of others.

GROUP SIZE
Any size.

HOME LINKS
Explain to parents and carers that it is better for them to demonstrate letter formation to their children using the hand that the child prefers to use.

Musical letters

What you need
CD player or tape recorder; music CD or tape; chair for each child; paper; pencil; sticky tape.

Preparation
Place the chairs, back to back, in two rows as you would for a game of 'Musical chairs'. Tape a piece of paper to the back of each chair with a lower-case letter written clearly on it.

What to do
Explain to the children that they are going to play a game of 'Musical chairs', but slightly different. Tell them that when the music plays, they must move around the chairs and that when it stops, they must sit down on the chair nearest to them. Explain that no chairs will be taken away, but that you will ask them to do something before the music begins again.

Start the music and stop it at a suitable point. When all the children are

seated, ask them to turn around and look at the letter that has been taped to the back of their chair. Explain that you are going to ask each of them in turn to name something beginning with the letter on the back of their chair.

Ask each child to tell you the letter sound and then to name something that begins with that sound before starting the music again.

Support and extension
Tell younger children their letter sound before you ask them to name something beginning with that letter. Ask older children to tell you their letter sound and its name before naming something, or ask them to think of two objects that begin with their letter.

Further ideas
■ Scatter large pieces of card with lower-case letters written on them around the floor. Ask the children to step from one 'stone' to another while the music plays. When the music stops, invite them to name something beginning with the letter on their 'stone'.
■ Encourage the children to move round the room like a baby. On cue, ask them to change their movements to those of a bear, and then back to a baby. Try other pairs of characters with the same initial sounds, such as dinosaur and dancer, runner and robot, and so on.

Hop, skip and dance

What you need
An outdoor space; chalk.

Preparation
Use a piece of chalk to write the letters 'r', 'w', 'd', 's' and 'h' in large lower case on the ground.

What to do
Show the children the letters that you have written on the ground. Tell them that they are going to move around each letter shape in a special way. Say that the way that they move will begin with the same sound as the sound made by their particular letter. Ask each of the children to go and stand by a letter.

Go through the letters, in turn, and ask the children to tell you the sound that each letter makes. As they tell you the sound that 'r' makes, for example, say, 'Yes, and you are going to "run" around the letter "r". Can you hear that "run" begins with the sound that "r" makes?'.

Use the following instructions for the letters: run around 'r', walk around 'w', dance around 'd', skip around 's' and hop around 'h'.

Before the children move, make sure that they are at the correct starting-point for each letter. Show them they will need to move twice over parts of the letters 'r', 'd' and 'h', the same way as when they are writing the letters. Now ask them to move around their letters in an appropriate manner. When they have done this, ask them to change letters.

Support and extension
Encourage younger children to move around one letter at a time, in turn, to reinforce both the sound and the particular direction of movement. Make sure that older children understand the movement for each letter at the beginning and then let them move from one letter to another without stopping.

Further ideas
■ Use a different set of letters and different movements, for example: crawl around 'c'; tiptoe around 't'; gallop around 'g'; leap along 'l'; march around 'm' and so on.
■ Ask the children to move around each letter and imitate an animal beginning with the same letter sound, for example, move around 'm' like a monkey.

Bake a letter

What you need
Pastry dough (enough for four children to each have a ball); aprons; flour; clean work surface or boards; greased baking trays; water; pencil; paper.

Preparation
Make the pastry dough or buy ready-made dough. Check for any food allergies and dietary requirements.

What to do
Give each child a ball of dough and explain that they are going to make some letter shapes to bake. Tell them that they are each going to make the letter that begins their first name. Explain that we use special letters at the beginning of names and that these are called capital letters.

Write the initial letter of each child's name on a piece of paper, and place it where the child can see it clearly as they work. As you write the letters, talk about the straight lines and curves in each letter, as appropriate.

Sprinkle some flour on the surface and demonstrate to the children how to roll the dough into 'rope' lengths before making their letters, emphasising that they should not press down as they roll the dough. Invite the children to make their 'ropes', then encourage them to form their initial letter on a greased baking tray. Show them how to pinch off the dough if a length is too long, and how to use a little water to bond two pieces of dough together.

Support and extension
Provide younger children with ready-rolled ropes of dough. Encourage older children to form the initial letter of their first name and second name.

Further ideas
■ Make letter shapes as presents for the children's family members, using the initial letters of their names.
■ Let the children make the lower-case version of their initial as well so that they can see how it differs from the capital letter.
■ Invite the children to roll out clay or Plasticine tiles and use a blunt pencil to mark their initial in them.

LEARNING OBJECTIVES
STEPPING STONE
Explore malleable materials by patting, stroking, poking, squeezing, pinching and twisting them.

EARLY LEARNING GOAL
Handle malleable materials safely and with increasing control.

GROUP SIZE
Four children.

HOME LINKS
Explain to parents and carers that it helps children to be able to recognise letters if they can touch and feel them. Encourage them to help their children make letter shapes with Plasticine or play dough.

Alphabet queue

What you need
An outdoor space; chalk.

Preparation
Write the whole alphabet in large capital letters on the ground with a piece of chalk.

What to do
Explain to the children that you would like them to queue up in a line in a special order. Ask them each to think about their first name, and the letter of the alphabet that it begins with. Say that they are going to use this letter to help them to queue up in alphabetical order.

Tell the children that you have chalked the alphabet on the ground to help them to queue in the correct order. Explain that when you say, 'Go!' they must hunt along the chalked alphabet to find the first letter of their first name and then stand on that letter. Say that if more than one person has a name beginning with the same letter, those people must stand side by side. Now invite the children to find their place in the queue.

Support and extension
Help younger children by talking about where the first letter of their first name comes in the alphabet. Encourage them to think whether it is near the beginning, middle or end of the alphabet to help them to find their place. Invite older children to make the queue several times while you time them to see if they can do it more quickly each time.

Further ideas
■ Play the game again, this time using the first letter of the children's second names to create a different order in the queue.
■ Write the alphabet in lower-case letters on the ground with chalk. Invite each child to choose a toy and encourage them to arrange the toys in alphabetical order on the chalked alphabet, thinking about the first letter sound in the toys' names, such as 't' for 'tractor' and 'teddy'.

Alphabet snake

What you need
The photocopiable sheet on page 78; thin card; dice; two counters.

Preparation
Copy the photocopiable sheet on to thin card.

What to do
Explain to the children that they are going to play a board game. Show them the alphabet snake. Draw their attention to the letters on each segment and ask if they notice anything about the order of these letters.

Tell the children that they are going to take turns to throw the dice and move their counters along the snake, starting at the letter 'a'. Explain that when they land on a letter, they must say the sound that the letter makes and then think of something that begins with that sound. Tell them that if they think of something, they can stay on that letter. If not, they must go back to where they were before. The first player to reach the letter 'z' is the winner.

Give each child a counter, decide who is going to start the game and begin.

Support and extension
Explain to younger children that when they land on a letter you will tell them the sound that this letter makes and that they must think of a word beginning with that sound. Ask older children to sound out and name the letter before giving a word.

Further ideas
■ Set aside a few minutes each day for 'alphabet time'. Focus on one letter per day and, using the letter sound, ask the children to think of as many words as possible beginning with that sound. Encourage the children to write down the appropriate letter.

■ Create a 'secret sound' bag. Place a number of objects beginning with the same sound into a bag. Invite the children to feel them without looking, then name each object and write the common initial letter.

■ Play the 'Alphabet snake' board game as above, but ask the children to think of a word ending with the sound of the letter that they land on.

One step forward

What you need
Four sheets of thin card; marker pen; sticky tape; large space.

Preparation
Write the letters 'f', 'b', 'r' and 'l' in large lower case, one on each sheet of card. Tape each sheet to one wall of the room. Bear in mind that 'f' = forwards, 'b' = backwards, 'r' = right and 'l' = left, and that this will represent the direction for the children who will be facing you.

What to do
Explain to the children that they are going to play a movement game. Say that you will tell them which way to move but you will not be using words, just a letter. Show them the letters on the walls. Talk about the letter 'f', writing the first sound in 'forwards'. Say, 'If you hear me say "f", you must move forwards'. Explain the other three letters in the same way. Help the children to understand the rules by trying out the four letters, asking them just to take one step in the correct direction.

Now explain to the children that you are going to say a letter and a number together, for example, if you say, 'r 4', they must go four steps to the right, of if you say, 'b 3', they should then take three steps backwards.

Support and extension
Stand with your back to younger children and hold your arm out to indicate the correct direction and model the movement each time. Challenge older children to remember two instructions at once, for example, 'r 2 then f 1'.

Further ideas
■ Use different letters to give the children instructions to stand **up**, sit **down** and turn **around**. Show them in quick succession for a short fun game.
■ Give each child a piece of paper and a pencil, and ask them to write the initial letter of actions that you are performing, for example 'r' for run, 'h' for hop, 'j' for jump and so on.

Letter mazes

What you need
The photocopiable sheet on page 79; coloured pencils.

Preparation
Copy the photocopiable sheet for each child.

What to do
Explain to the children that they are going to find their way through each of the mazes using a coloured pencil. Invite them to choose the colour that they would like to use.

Check that each child is holding the pencil in a tripod grip. The thumb and forefinger should be on either side of the pencil, with the pencil resting on the middle finger, near the first joint.

Point out the arrow showing the way into each maze and explain to the children that they should start here. Make sure that they understand that there is only one way through the maze and that they cannot cross over any lines. Show them the arrow where they should come out of the maze. Invite them to start the first maze.

When the children have completed the first maze, ask them to look carefully at the line that they have drawn. Point out that it forms the shape of a letter and invite them to tell you the name of the letter shape they have made.

Let the children complete the other two mazes, asking each time which letter shape they have drawn.

Support and extension
Draw a dotted line for younger children to trace over. Invite older children to tell you what they have drawn before you talk about the letter shapes.

Further ideas
■ Use building blocks to create large-scale tracks in the shape of letters and let the children manipulate toy vehicles through these 'roads'.
■ Stick pipe-cleaners or string to pieces of card to make track lines in the shape of various letters. Let the children trace their finger through the tracks before attempting to write the relevant letters on paper.
■ Cut out letter shapes from pieces of card and create tactile letters, for example, stick cotton wool on to a 'c', self-adhesive dots on to a 'd', buttons on a 'b' and so on. Use items for each letter linked to its sound.

Creative development

This chapter suggests a range of ideas to help children recognise and explore sounds and songs, and to match movement to music, as well as exploring shape, form and texture in two- or three-dimensions while using their imagination in art and design, music, dance, stories and role-play.

Nursery names

What you need
A selection of nursery rhymes with character names in the title.

What to do
Explain to the children that you are going to sing some nursery rhymes together. Tell them that you have chosen some rhymes that are named after one or more of the characters in them. Start with 'Jack and Jill' and encourage the children join in with singing it.

When the children have finished singing, ask them to listen very carefully as you say the names of the two people in the rhyme, and especially to the sounds at the beginning of the two names. Ask them whether the sounds at the beginning of the names are the same or not.

Now invite the children to sing 'Little Boy Blue' with you. When you have finished say, 'Now, listen to the name "Boy Blue". Do these two words have the same sound at the beginning?'.

Say some more nursery rhymes that have a character with an alliterative name, such as 'Little Miss Muffet', 'Little Tommy Tucker' and 'Lucy Locket'. Then begin to intersperse examples in which the main character does not have a name beginning with the same sound, for example, 'Little Bo Peep' and 'Little Jack Horner'.

Support and extension
Help younger children to hear the first sound in names by separating the first sound out for them to compare. After you have sung 'Little Boy Blue' together, invite older children to think of some nursery rhyme characters whose two names begin with the same first sound.

Further ideas
■ Explore the children's own names to see whether their first name and second name begin with the same sound or if any children share the same sound at the beginning of their first names or second names.
■ Make a collection of pictures of famous people and cartoon characters from newspapers and magazines and help the children to find out which ones have first and second names beginning with the same sound.
■ Ask the children to draw pictures of nursery rhyme characters with alliterative names. Display them with labels, on which the initial letters of the two names are written in a different colour.

Slither like a snake

What you need
A large space.

What to do
Tell the children that you are going to read a rhyme and that you would like them to listen very carefully to the sounds that they hear.

S-s-s-slither like a snake without a sound.
W-w-w-wiggle like a worm along the ground.
H-h-h-hop like a hare, hop really high.
C-c-c-creep like a cat, cunning and sly.

Now talk to the children about the rhyme. Ask them to listen to the words 'slither' and 'snake'. Emphasise the first sound in each word and draw the children's attention to the fact that the sound at the beginning of the movement word, and the sound at the beginning of the animal name, are the same. Read down the rhyme and repeat the other movement words and animal names together.

Invite the children to find a large space. Encourage them to listen to the rhyme again and to move like the animal in each line as you read it. Tell them that as soon as they hear the first sound, they should start moving like that particular animal. Say, for example, 'Remember, as soon as you hear s-s-s, you know it will be a snake, so begin to slither'.

Support and extension
Help younger children by pausing after making the initial sound and checking that they know which way to move. Do not point out the common initial sound to older children, but ask them what they notice about the words, for example, 'slither' and 'snake'.

Further ideas
■ Change the order of the lines but still maintain a rhyme, for example, read lines four, three, two, one or lines two, one, four, three. Challenge the children to use the initial sound to cue them to the next movement.
■ Read other rhymes to the children with alliterative movement words such as 'Run, rabbit, run'.
■ Encourage the children to think of some alliterative movement words for different animals.

LEARNING OBJECTIVES
STEPPING STONE
Respond to sound with body movement.

EARLY LEARNING GOAL
Recognise repeated sounds and sound patterns and match movements to music.

GROUP SIZE
Any size.

HOME LINKS
Send home a copy of the rhyme and ask parents and carers to read it to their children so that they can show them how they can move in response to each line.

Sun, sea and sand

What you need
Paper; paint; paintbrushes; aprons.

What to do
Explain to the children that they are going to paint a special picture. Tell them that you are going to ask them some questions and that each time they say the correct answer to a question, they can add something to their picture.

Ask the children to think about water. Then say, 'Can you think of some water that you would see at the beach? It is salty and has waves in it'. When the children have answered, 'sea', invite them to paint the sea across the middle of their picture.

Work through the following questions, each time asking the children to add their answer to the picture.
■ What else can you see at the beach that is yellow and made of lots of tiny grains? (Sand.)
■ You have painted the sea and sand, what do you think would be above both of these? (The sky.)
■ What might be shining in the sky? (The sun.)
■ What sort of bird might you see in the sky at the seaside? (Seagull.)
■ What could you build with the sand? (Sandcastle.)
Now list all the things that the children have painted. Ask them to listen to the sound at the beginning of each word and tell you what they notice.

LEARNING OBJECTIVES
STEPPING STONE
Work creatively on a large or small scale.

EARLY LEARNING GOAL
Explore colour, texture, shape, form and space in two or three dimensions.

GROUP SIZE
Up to five children.

Support and extension
Before younger children start to paint, tell them that everything that they are going to paint begins with the same sound. With the older children, make a list of what they have painted and ask if they notice anything about each of the words.

Further ideas
■ Create other paintings with different items that all share the same initial sound, for example, a garden with a bat, ball, boat and balloon or a field with a fence, flowers, frog and fly.
■ Make 'sound' collages of materials that all begin with the same sound, for example, string, sand, sticky tape, sequins and silk.
■ Invite the children to paint a letter then decorate it with small stickers of images that begin with that letter, for example, stars on an 's', dots on a 'd' or hearts on an 'h'.

HOME LINKS
Ask parents and carers to contribute different materials to provide a resource for 'sound' collages.

Alphabet dance

What you need

A CD player or tape recorder; CD or music tape; large space.

What to do

Explain to the children that you are going to play some music for them to dance to. Start the music and encourage the children to dance freely for a few minutes. Then stop the music and explain that you would now like them to dance like different people or animals.

Start the music again. Call out 'astronaut' and encourage the children to dance like an astronaut. When they have done this for a few minutes, call out other names, for example, ballerina, clown, dinosaur and elephant.

As you name each person or animal, ask the children if they can tell you the letter at the beginning of that name. Repeat the names of all five characters and name the letters, then ask them if they can notice anything about these letters.

Support and extension

Stop the music between the characters for younger children, and demonstrate how to dance to each one. Encourage them to say the sounds at the beginning of the characters' names, then tell them the letter names. Do not name the initial letters for older children. Simply recap the names and ask them if they can notice anything about the first letters in the five names.

Further ideas

■ Encourage the children to work through the alphabet by suggesting characters that they could dance like for the letters 'f', 'g', 'h', 'I' and 'j'. Use questions to prompt them to suggest a fox, gorilla, a hippopotamus, an insect and a juggler.

■ Play music such as *The Flight of the Bumble Bee* by Rimsky-Korsakov or excerpts from *The Carnival of the Animals* by Saint Saëns. Give a letter clue to the animal being represented by the music, and ask the children which animal they think it is.

Letter pictures

What you need
Paper; paint (including black); paintbrushes.

What to do
Give each child a piece of paper and a paintbrush. Ask the children to paint a large letter 'h' in the middle of the paper in black paint. Model this if necessary.

Now ask the children which sound this letter writes. If they are having difficulty telling you, say that it is the sound that comes at the beginning of the word 'house'. Tell the children that you are going to help them to turn the letter 'h' into a picture of a house so they can remember its sound. Let them choose the contrasting colour paint that they would like to use to make the rest of the picture of the house.

Give the children step-by-step instructions, saying, 'Paint a line along the bottom of the letter to make the bottom of the house. Make the part of the letter that sticks up into a chimney. Paint a small line across to make the top of the chimney, and another line down to make the other side of the chimney. Paint a door and some windows on the house'.

Support and extension
Help younger children by painting the basic letter shape for them, and modelling how to turn this into the picture of a house. Encourage older children to make their own suggestions as to what they could add to the letter to turn it into a house.

Further ideas
■ Invite the children to turn other letters into pictures, for example, 'b' into a boot; 'c' into a caterpillar; 'a' into an apple and 'l' into a leg.
■ Encourage the children to build letter shapes using construction materials and explore which letters are easier or more difficult to create in this way.

LEARNING OBJECTIVES
STEPPING STONE
Pretend that one object represents another, especially when objects have characteristics in common.

EARLY LEARNING GOAL
Use their imagination in art and design, music, dance, imaginative and role-play and stories.

GROUP SIZE
Up to four children.

HOME LINKS
Let the children take their paintings home and ask parents and carers to discuss why particular letters have been chosen as a basis for particular objects with their children. Explain the link with the initial sound, so that parents and carers can ask appropriate questions.

Letter prints

**LEARNING
OBJECTIVES
STEPPING STONE**
Differentiate marks
and movements on
paper.

**EARLY LEARNING
GOAL**
Explore colour,
texture, shape, form,
and space in two or
three dimensions.

GROUP SIZE
Three children.

What you need
A5 tracing paper; Swiss-roll tins; trays or other smooth, washable surface; thick paint; aprons.

Preparation
Spread a thin layer of undiluted paint over the base of the tins or trays.

What to do
Explain to the children that they are going to create a pattern using the first letter of their name. Invite each child, in turn, to tell you the initial letter of their name. Ask them to show you how to write that letter by tracing it on the table using the forefinger of their writing hand.

Give each child a tray of paint and ask them to write the initial letter in the paint using the same finger that they used to trace on the table. Suggest that they press the end of their finger quite flat into the paint to make a wide track through it. When they have written their initial, make sure that the children wash their hands.

Let the children place a piece of tracing paper over the paint and help them to smooth over it very gently with their fingertips. Move out from the letter shape and do not exert pressure or the letter pattern will disappear. Carefully lift one corner of the paper and peel off the pattern, then leave the letters to dry.

Finally, display the letters on a window to let the light shine through them.

Support and extension
Help younger children by modelling their initial letter and guiding their finger in the paint. Challenge older children to form repeated letters of the same size in rows.

HOME LINKS
Explain to parents
and carers how
writing letters in
paint, sand or salt
helps children to
become familiar
with letter shapes
before using a pencil.
Encourage them to
try this with their
children at home.

Further ideas
■ Make 'reverse' patterns to display alongside the children's original patterns. Encourage them to paint their initial letter on a piece of tracing paper, using the same colour paint. Ask them to make the letters the same size, and put them in the same place as on their print pattern.
■ Let the children make the initial letter of their name in the sand tray, then suggest that they press shells into the pattern.

Old MacDonald

What you need
The song 'Old MacDonald Had a Farm' (Traditional); pieces of card (10cm²); marker pen.

Preparation
Write the initial lower-case letter of a farm animal's name from the song on each piece of card.

What to do
Tell the children that you are going to sing a song together. If the children are not familiar with the song 'Old MacDonald Had a Farm', practise the first verse with them and explain how to sing further verses by adding an extra animal and making the noise of each animal in turn. Sing two verses and tell the children which animal to include next.

Now say that you are going to sing several verses of the song again. Tell the children that, this time, you are not going to say which animal comes next in each verse. Explain that you are going to hold up a card with a letter on it. Say that you want them to look at the letter and to suggest an animal that begins with that letter to include in the next verse. Sing one verse of the song to make sure that the children understand the idea. Then proceed with several verses.

Support and extension
When you hold up the cards, make the letter sound to help younger children and prompt them with several animal names. Invite them to choose the one that has this sound at the beginning. Let older children choose an animal and write the initial letter on a card themselves. Ask them to hold up their cards in turn to prompt the next verse of the song.

LEARNING OBJECTIVES
STEPPING STONE
Sing a few simple, familiar songs.

EARLY LEARNING GOAL
Recognise and explore how sounds can be changed, sing simple songs from memory.

GROUP SIZE
Any size.

Further ideas
■ Broaden the scope of animals, and possible initial letters, by singing 'Old Macdonald's Zoo'.
■ Use the same idea to play 'I Went to Market'. Ask the children to add to the list by suggesting items that could be bought, in response to a letter card.

HOME LINKS
Explain the activity to parents and carers and ask them to sing the song in the same way at home with their children.

Feel the letter

STEPPING STONE
Further explore an experience using a range of senses.

EARLY LEARNING GOAL
Respond in a variety of ways to what they see hear, smell, touch and feel.

GROUP SIZE
Three children.

What you need
A set of wooden or plastic lower-case alphabet letters; tea towels.

What to do
Ask the children to sit at a table and give each child a wooden or plastic letter. As you do so, name the letter and say, for example, 'I would like you to hold this letter "b"'. Now ask each child in turn to feel the letter and to talk to you about its shape. Encourage them to think about where it feels straight, where it is bumpy and so on.

Take the letters back and invite each child to place their hands on the table in front of them. Cover each child's hands with a tea towel and explain that they are going to play a game with the letters.

Invite the children to close their eyes and then place two letters under each tea towel. Each time, include the letter that each child has just handled. Tell each child that you would like them to give you the letter that they held before but that they must decide which letter is the correct one by just feeling it and not looking at it. Ask them to say, 'The letter that I want is …' and name the letter that they felt before. Then encourage the children to pull out the letter that they think is correct.

Support and extension
Help younger children by describing again how the letter felt before. Give older children three letters to choose between.

Further ideas
■ Play the game without letting the children feel one of the letters first. Simply name which letter you would like and ask them to tell you what it should feel like before they touch the letters and make their decision.
■ Dip a marble in thick paint and ask the children to see if they can roll it around in a letter shape on a piece of paper.
■ Write letters with your finger on the children's palms or backs, and ask them to name the letter that you wrote.

HOME LINKS
Explain to parents and carers that by encouraging their children to touch and feel letters, it will be easier for them to learn the shapes that they need to write.

Texture letters

What you need
Pieces of card (10cm²); marker pen; glue; string; cotton wool; pipe-cleaners; sand; plastic washing-up bowl.

Preparation
Write a different large lower-case letter on each piece of card. Put the sand in the washing-up bowl.

What to do
Give each child a piece of card and ask them to trace their finger around the letter. Model this for them and talk about the shape of the letter as you trace around it and the movements that you are using. Explain that it would be much easier to feel the letter if it stood out from the card. Tell the children that they are going to make their letter stand out.

Show the children the string, cotton wool, pipe-cleaners and sand, and invite them to choose what they would like to use to make their own letters stand out. When the children have selected the items, show them how to place glue along the letter shape. Now ask them to put their chosen material along the glue line. When the glue has dried, let them gently feel the letter, tracing their finger around it, as before. Encourage them to think of things that begin with that letter sound.

Support and extension
Help younger children by applying the glue for them and restricting their choice of textured materials to cotton wool or sand. Let older children write their own letters on the cards.

■■■■■■■■■■■■■■■■■■■■

Further ideas
■ Make a selection of different-textured letters. When the glue is dry, paper-clip pieces of paper over the cards and let the children use wax crayons and paper to make a rubbing of the letters. Ask them to draw something beginning with that letter.
■ Invite the children to close their eyes and present them with a textured letter. Let them feel the letter and encourage them to decide which letter they think it is.
■ Stick small self-adhesive dots around a letter shape and let the children feel them with their eyes closed. Talk about how Braille letters help blind people to read.

LEARNING OBJECTIVES
STEPPING STONE
Begin to describe the texture of things.

EARLY LEARNING GOAL
Explore colour, texture, shape, form and space in two or three dimensions.

■■■■■■■■■■■

GROUP SIZE
Up to five children.

■■■■■■■■■■■

HOME LINKS
Ask parents and carers to encourage their children to 'guess a letter' by using plastic fridge-magnet letters at home.

■■■■■■■■■■■

Colour the dots

LEARNING OBJECTIVES
STEPPING STONE
Begin to differentiate colours.

EARLY LEARNING GOAL
Explore colour, texture, shape, form, and space in two or three dimensions.

GROUP SIZE
Four or five children.

What you need
The photocopiable sheet on page 80; wax crayons, coloured pencils or felt-tipped pens.

Preparation
Copy the photocopiable sheet for each child.

What to do
Give each child a copy of the photocopiable sheet and explain that they are going to colour some puzzle pictures. Tell them that they are going to use only one colour for each puzzle.

Ask the children to look carefully at the first picture on their sheet. Explain that they are only going to colour the shapes that have a dot on them. Say that you would like them to use the colour yellow and invite them to colour the dotted shapes on this picture.

Now ask them to look very carefully at what they have coloured. Explain that they should be able to see a letter shape and ask which letter they think they have coloured.

Remind the children that they have coloured the letter 'y' in yellow. Ask what sound comes at the beginning of the word 'yellow' and which letter writes that sound.

Continue with the other pictures, encouraging the children to use orange for the second picture, red for the third and green for the final picture. Help them to work out the link between the resulting letter and the sound at the beginning of each colour word.

Support and extension
Explain to younger children that they are colouring the letter 'y' in yellow because 'y' writes the first sound of that word, rather than asking them to work it out. Ask older children why they think that you have asked them to colour the letters in particular colours.

HOME LINKS
Ask parents and carers to encourage colouring activities for their children. Explain that these will help them to develop the small hand and finger movements needed for writing letters.

Further ideas
■ Create similar puzzle pictures for the initial letters of other colours, such as 'p' for purple or pink, 'b' for blue or brown and so on.
■ When the children have finished colouring the letters, glue the finished pictures on to thin card. Invite the children to cut the letters into pieces, along the lines, to create their own set of letter puzzles.

Animal names

Photocopy on to card, cut out the pictures and match the initial sounds.

Hide the animal

Photocopy on to card, cut out the pictures and match the initial sounds.

Fishing fun

Rhyming words

Word detectives

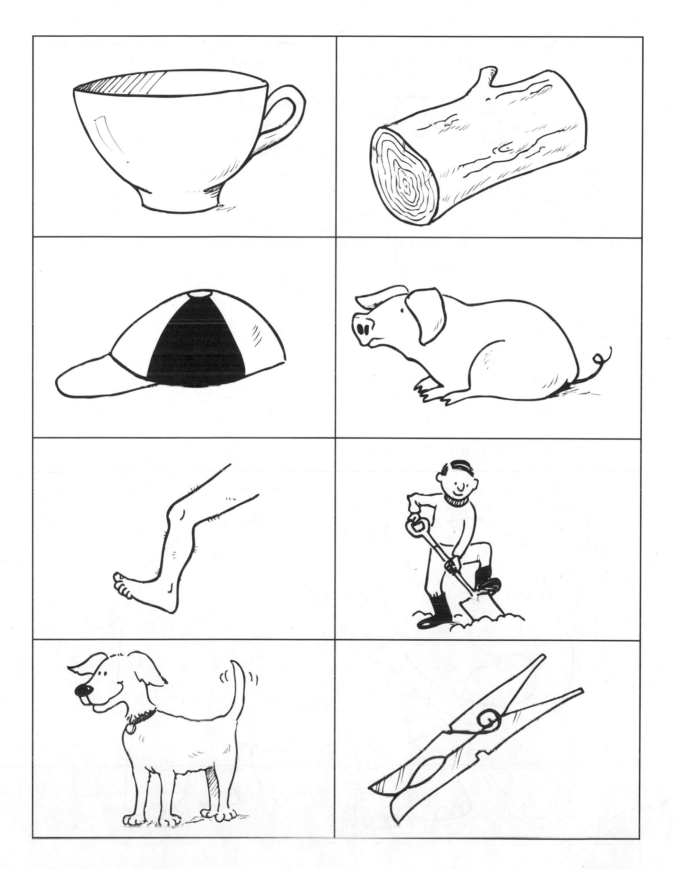

Simple puzzle

Use this picture for the a, b, c, d sequence.

Use this picture for the e, f, g, h sequence.

Letter shapes

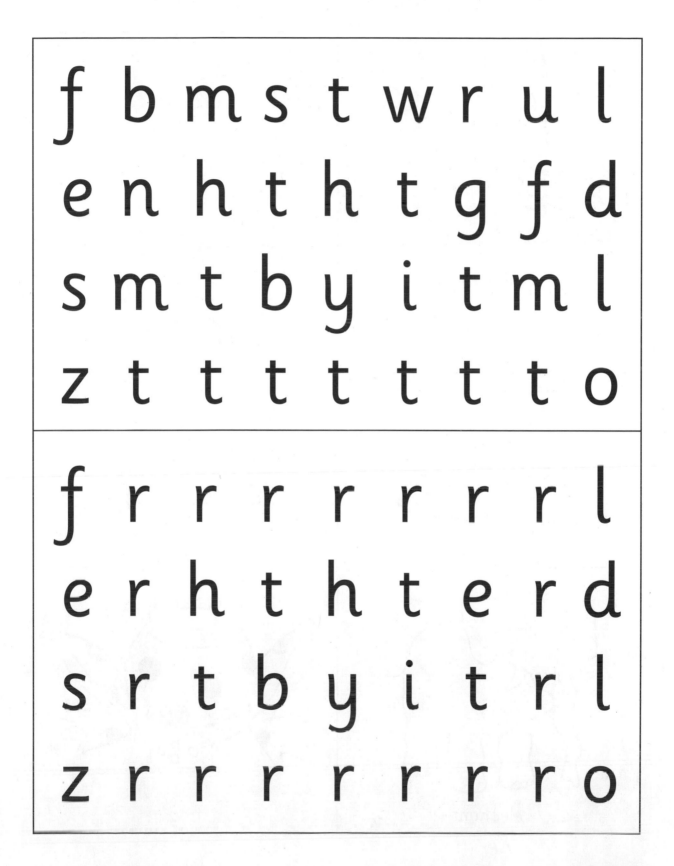

f b m s t w r u l
e n h t h t g f d
s m t b y i t m l
z t t t t t t t o

f r r r r r r r l
e r h t h t e r d
s r t b y i t r l
z r r r r r r r o

Animal a–z (1)

alligator

bear

crocodile

dog

elephant

frog

Animal a–z (2)

goat	hippo
iguana	jaguar
kangaroo	lion

Animal a–z (3)

monkey

newt

ostrich

panda

quail

rabbit

Animal a–z (4)

snake	tiger
umbrella bird	vole
whale	fox
yak	zebra

Snake game

Throw a dice and move the counter up the snake.
Make the letter sound and think of a word that begins with the letter.

Follow the letters

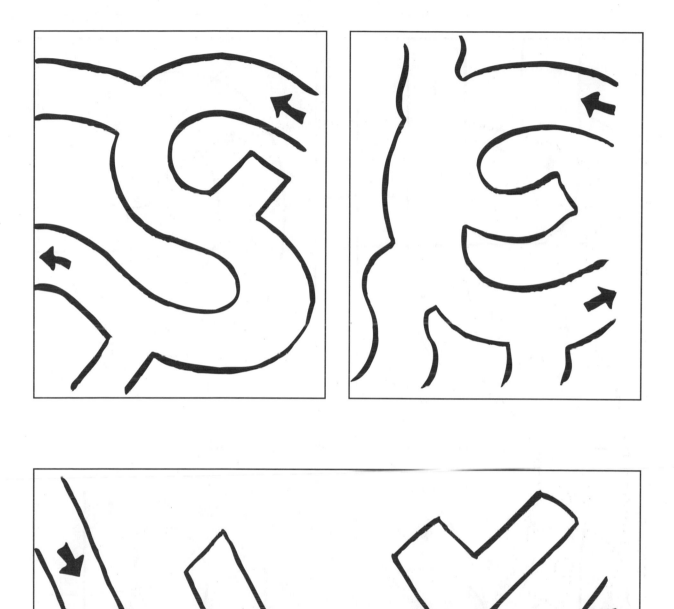

 79

Colourful letters